WORKBOOK
For
INTERCULTURAL ENCOUNTERS

The Fundamentals of Intercultural Communication

Fifth Edition

Donald W. Klopf

West Virginia University (Professor Emeritus)

University of Hawaii (Professor Emeritus)

Morton Publishing Company

925 W. Kenyon Ave., Unit 12

Englewood, Colorado 80110

http://www.morton-pub.com

Printed in the United States of America

ISBN: 0-89582-553-8

Contents

**Bring This Workbook
To Each Class Session**

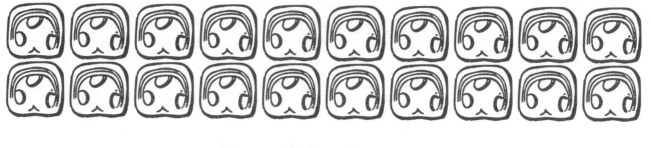

Syllabus

The Textbook

Intercultural Encounters addresses cultural differences and their effects on communication. The book's content reflects the pluralistic nature of today's society. With its ethnic mix and diversity of cultures, knowledge of intercultural communication is vital for people to interact satisfactorily with others.

Although this text will not solve international problems, it should go a long way toward making readers more sensitive to the communication styles of people from other cultures with whom they interact. This should result in insights relevant to intercultural interaction — matters pertaining to cultural and subcultural differences in the realm of communication.

Among the topics covered are communication and its process, culture and its universal characteristics, and how communication and culture interrelate. Perception — the key to successful intercultural communication — is addressed from a crosscultural perspective.

Basic to understanding the people who communicate interculturally is knowledge of their needs, values, beliefs, and attitudes. The text pays special attention to three attitudes that have a negative impact on talk across cultures: ethnocentrism, stereotyping, and prejudice. The two basic means of communication — verbal and nonverbal— are discussed in terms of their basic elements and the challenges they raise in intercultural talk. Social structure plays a vital role in a culture. It is studied here with regard to the institutions and relationships created by the family educational systems, religion, government, and financial systems. The book addresses culture shock along with the process of becoming acculturated.

Throughout the book, communication behaviors and cultural patterns of various subcultural and cultural groups are introduced for illustration and comparison. Cultural dissimilarities are exemplified to highlight the contrast vividly.

The Workbook

Designed as an adjunct to the textbook, the *Workbook* provides a series of exercises that apply information from the text. Concluding each topical component is an exercise entitled "What Does It Mean?" These exercises test your knowledge of key terms used in the text.

The first exercise sets forth the term project — preparation of a cultural resume. It is intended to provide an in-depth look at a specific culture, a synopsis of the culture and its communication. An example of a cultural resume is included.

Several of the other exercises support the term project. These require a closer look at an intercultural concept — for instance, language — as it relates specifically to the culture being studied for the resume. For each of these exercises, an example is included. The examples are from Asian cultures, as these differ most widely from the predominant culture of the United States and thus portray the concept most vividly.

The instructor will assign the exercises. Some may be the topics of group discussions or group projects. Others will be completed outside of class. Because some exercises will be reviewed in class, students should bring the *Workbook* to each class session.

PERSONAL DATA FORM

Please print and complete all information.

Course Name and Number: _____

Name: _____

Social Security Number: _____

Local Address: _____

Local Telephone Number: _____

Permanent Home Address: _____

_____

Permanent Home Telephone Number: _____

Major: _____

Communication Courses Taken: _____

_____

Some students prefer speaking over writing; some prefer writing over speaking; some have no preference. Which do you prefer? (Check one.)

Speaking: _____   Writing: _____   No Preference: _____

I have read the course syllabus and understand all of its provisions.

Date: _____   Signed: _____

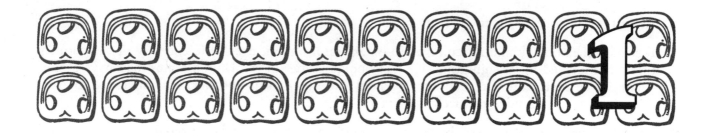

Cultural Resumé

A resumé is a summing up of something. Exercise 1 involves summing up a culture. The exercise requires that you prepare a resumé of a culture, following the instructions below. The Cultural Resumé is due on the date indicated, roughly at the end of the term, giving you sufficient time to complete one like the sample included.

Objectives

- To encourage you to become familiar with a specific culture as you summarize its unique customs, traditions, values, and lifestyles
- To help you develop a sensitivity toward the people of the culture you choose to study, enabling you to communicate better with people from that culture

Reference

Chapter 1 of text

Instructions

Completion time: (per instructor)

1. From the list below, choose a country to study.

Algeria	Finland	Mexico	Scotland
Argentina	France	Netherlands	Singapore
Australia	Germany	New Zealand	South Africa
Austria	Greece	Nigeria	Spain
Belgium	Hong Kong	Norway	Sri Lanka
Bolivia	Hungary	Pakistan	Sweden
Brazil	India	Paraguay	Switzerland
Bulgaria	Indonesia	Peru	Syria
Canada	Iran	Philippines	Tahiti
Chile	Ireland	Poland	Taiwan
Czechoslovakia	Israel	Portugal	Thailand
Denmark	Italy	Puerto Rico	Turkey
Egypt	Jordan	Romania	Wales
England	Kenya	Russia	Yugoslavia
Ethiopia	Lebanon	Samoa	Zaire
Fiji	Malaysia	Saudi Arabia	Zimbabwe

2. Report your choice to the instructor.

3. Research the country and its culture. To obtain information, check the embassy of the country (most are located in Washington, DC; metropolitan cities in the United States may have a consulate office representing the country), school and other local libraries, Human Relation Area Files, and computer-aided research systems.

4. Organize useful answers for the following items, which should be covered in your Cultural Resumé.

   A. **Customs and Courtesies**

Greetings	Gestures	Traveling
Visiting	Personal appearance	Communicating
Eating	Group meetings	interpersonally

   B. **The People**

General attitudes and values	Religion
Population	Holidays, religious and political
Language	

   C. **Lifestyle**

Family	Work
Dating, courtship, and marriage	Recreation
Social and economic levels	Food

   D. **The Nation**

History and government	Transportation and communication systems
Educational system	Health, sanitation, and medical facilities
Land and climate	Scale map of the country (placement can vary —
Economy	see Sample)

   F. **Communication Style**

   G. **Bibliography**

5. Complete your answers using the format in the accompanying sample as a guide. Write simply, directly, and tightly, summarizing in several pages the information requested in step 4.

The instructor may request progress reports periodically.

Sample Cultural Resumé

JAPAN

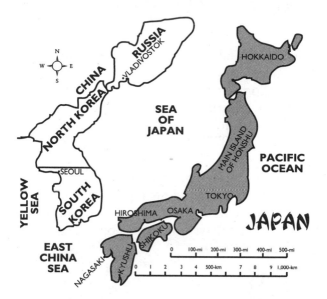

Customs and Courtesies

Greetings

Typically, the Japanese bow to greet friends, pay respects, express thanks, apologize, ask favors, and say goodbye. The depth of the bow and the number of times repeated indicate the relationship between the two parties.

Visiting

The Japanese slip off their shoes when entering the house (and temples and shrines). They bring wrapped gifts when visiting someone, the host opens the gifts after the guests leave. Guests admire the host's flower arrangements or art with quiet appreciation rather than verbal compliments.

Men lead the way into rooms. If seated, they do not rise when being introduced to women. Men are introduced first; the elders are first, and the women follow. Thank-you notes are sent promptly after the visit. When visiting, people from other cultures are expected to wear their own usual clothes, not Japanese attire.

Eating

Chopsticks often are used when eating. These are laid down uncrossed or are left sticking in food. When eating from a bowl, such as when eating rice, the bowl is held chest-high or close to the mouth and the food is more or less shoveled in. If knives and forks are used, they usually are handled European style. Food purchased at a streetside snack stand is eaten at the stand, not carried and eaten along the way as people in the United States often do.

Gestures

The Japanese do not use conspicuous gestures such as waving their hands and arms when talking. They sit at tables with both feet flat on the floor. They sometimes sit on the floor, crossing their legs under them. While sitting, they do not put their legs on something like a desk or a table. Laughter is quiet and refined. Yawning in public is frowned upon, as is chewing gum in public.

Personal Appearance

Men usually wear suits and ties in public, although in summer they remove their coats. Women wear modest dresses. They avoid conspicuous colors, strong perfumes, and heavy make-up or fancy hair-dos. They conform to the rest of the people and do not want to stand out.

Group Meetings

Decisions usually are the result of considerable interpersonal interaction taking place over a long time and involving all of the people who will be affected by the decision. Business dealings with new associates are initiated in conversations over tea, sake, or golf, not with the expectation of completing a transaction but, instead, with the purpose of getting to know the other person first. The Japanese proceed cautiously, looking for weaknesses and strengths, in a fairly formal sort of atmosphere.

Traveling

Japan has many historical sites and interesting places to visit. In the South the country resembles Hawaii. In the North it is like northern mountainous regions in the USA. Excellent transportation is available, and lots of lodging facilities. Hotels are Western-style with bathrooms, and bedrooms with beds. Japanese-style inns (ryokan) usually have no beds (people sleep on futons on the floor) or bathrooms (bathing areas are shared in common).

Communicating Interpersonally

Politeness is reflected in a low voice, quiet laughter, respect for age, and no public displays of affection. The Japanese avoid loud conversations in public places and do not call across a lobby, room, or hallway. They are quiet and discreet.

The People

General Attitudes and Values

Japanese people are characterized by discipline, and politeness. Group harmony is the norm in their familiar social relationships. The Japanese recognize three basic kinds of people: those they know well, those they are acquainted with, and strangers or "those who don't exist." With the first two groups the relationships are clearly defined. Caught in an unusual situation, the Japanese wonder, "What am I expected to do next?" In contrast, an American would ask, "What *will* I do next?"

The Japanese are extremely sensitive to what others think or expect of them. This awareness of other people's opinions and expectations guides their behavior. "Giri" — meaning obligation and duty — underlies their hierarchical system of how one stands in association with another. Earnestness, austerity, and tension must have an outlet, and bars, restaurants, and cabarets provide the outlet, at least for the men. Their attitudes and values resemble a tapestry; no one thread stands out. The whole is superior to the parts; towering individuals are mistrusted. Everything functions smoothly as a melded, interwoven whole.

Population

With a population of roughly 120 million, about 3% of the world's total population and approximately 60% of the population of the USA, Japan is the 17th most densely populated country in the world with 767 people per square mile (by comparison, the USA has 58 to the square mile). The population is 99% homogeneous, with a small number of Koreans, Chinese, and native Ainu. Tokyo is the second largest city in the world. The average life span is 69 years for men and 74 for women.

Language

The official language is Japanese. Many Japanese are conversant also in English, Spanish, or French, and all middle- and high-school students have to study English. Written Japanese has similarities to Chinese ideographs, and the Japanese use two phonetic alphabets (*hiragana* and *katagana*) as simplified versions of the Chinese ideographs.

Religion

Buddhism and Shintoism are the main religions, and many of the people profess more than one religion. They may practice Shinto marriages and Buddhist funerals, for example. Christianity enrolls only a small fraction of the population.

Holidays

New Year's is the biggest holiday of the year, when most businesses close for three or four days while the people visit relatives, temples, or take trips. Other holidays include Adults' Day (Jan. 15), National Foundation Day (Feb. 11), Emperor's Birthday (April 9), Constitution Day (May 3), Children's Day (May 5), Senior Citizens Day (Sept. 15), Physical Athletic Day (Oct. 10), Culture Day (Nov. 3), and Labor Thanksgiving Day (Nov. 23).

Lifestyle

The Family

Although the aged parents still live with their married children in many instances, the trend is away from the traditional, large, multigeneration family. Families are most apt to be nuclear, with husband and wife and one or two children. The abortion rate is the third highest in the world; roughly 35% of all pregnancies are aborted. The suicide rate is the tenth highest in the world.

Dating, Courtship, and Marriage

Dating is a relatively recent practice, becoming popular during the last decade. Dating begins at age 17 or 18. Marriage takes place when men are about 27 years old and women marry at a slightly younger age. In the past, marriages were arranged by elder friends of the family or go-betweens. Nowadays the couple usually decides whether they will marry.

Social and Economic Levels

Monthly wages equate to about $1500–$2500 in U.S. dollars, but semiannual bonuses raise these figures considerably, bringing the typical wage almost to the USA level. After graduation, the highest hurdle for a Japanese person is getting the first job, which normally is selected with care. Once hired, the employee probably will stay with the company for life, considering resignation only in the most dire circumstances. Little short of an outright crime will persuade the company to fire an employee. Employees receive fringe benefits such as health insurance, welfare pension plan, unemployment and accident insurance, and dependents' allowance. Employees often live in company housing, make purchases at a company store, and receive loans from the company.

Work

Usually the work week is 5½ to 6 days. Employees are on time, are rarely absent, and mind their manners. Promotions are based on seniority, not ability. Retirement is at age 55, although this has changed to 60 for most men today. Typically, the wage earner owns a television set, a washer, a refrigerator, and a few other household luxuries. Thriftiness is important, and the average wage earner saves about 20% of the salary — in bank accounts, not stocks or bonds.

Recreation

Most Western-type sports — baseball, soccer, volleyball, tennis, skiing, jogging, and golf — are popular in Japan. Football is gaining more and more interest. The traditional sports, such as sumo wrestling, judo, kendo, and karate, remain popular. The people enjoy movies and television as well as the traditional theater styles of *noh* and *kabuki*. Sightseeing is a national pastime, and overnight trips are common.

Food

Average Japanese meals are different from Western fare. The breakfast menu consists of items such as rice, bean-paste soup, pickled vegetables, seaweed, and perhaps fermented soybeans. If lunch is eaten away from home, it is a lunch box of cold rice, pickled vegetables, and a bite of fish, or a bowl of noodles or rice curry. At home, lunch consists of breakfast leftovers. The dinner menu consists of clear soup, rice, fish, pickled vegetables, and seaweed. The average Japanese person has rice at least twice a day. Japanese tea usually accompanies meals.

Dining out and for special occasions, Japanese people eat sukiyaki (a dish cooked at the table, consisting of green vegetables, onions, thinly sliced beef, and bean-curd), tempura (deep-fried, batter-dipped fish, and vegetables), yaki-tori (barbecued chicken on skewers), sushi (rice wrapped in seaweed with a center of vegetable or fish), and soba noodles. Sake, a rice wine, is the national drink.

The Nation

History and Government

According to mythology, the Japanese people were created by the union of two gods, as the country itself was created by divine inspiration. Japanese scholars, however, believe that the race was created by separate streams arriving, for the one, from Polynesia via southern Indonesia and the Philippines, and, for the other, from Mongolia via China and Korea. In any event, the Japanese are remarkably homogeneous in appearance and attitudes. The present emperor, Akihito, is the son of Hirohito.

Military clans held power from the 12th century through the 19th century, even with emperors on the throne. Since the end of World War II, Japan has been a constitutional monarchy, resembling an American-style parliamentary arrangement within a British-style framework. Two houses of parliament (the Diet) — the House of Representatives and the House of Councillors — function like the U.S. Congress. The lower house elects a prime minister, who runs the country with the help of a cabinet, which he selects.

Educational System

Since 1947, the 6–3–3–4 system of education has been in force: 6 years of compulsory primary school, 3 years of compulsory middle school, 3 years of high school, and 4 years of university. Postgraduate school is 2 years for the master's course and 3 years for the doctoral course. Attendance at the compulsory levels is almost 100% (99.9%).

The country has about 380 four-year universities and about 475 two-year colleges. Entrance into the university is by exam, and only one in every five to 15 students is admitted. Even so, approximately 2 million students go to the universities. The school year begins in April, the second term after the July-August summer holidays, and the third term after the winter holidays at the year's end. In March a spring break precedes the new school year. Besides the regular schools, many special private schools teach subjects such as calligraphy, sewing, cooking, dancing, flower arranging, tea ceremony, automobile driving, and so on.

Land and Climate

Nihon or Nippon (Japanese for Japan) is an archipelago made up of four main islands and 3,326 smaller islands (maximum width, 170 miles) extending north and south 1500 miles. Tokyo is located on Honshu, the main island. The total area is slightly smaller than California. More than 90% consists of mountains, many of which are active volcanoes.

Central Japan's climate is like that of northern California. Northern Japan's climate is similar to that of New England. Southern Japan's climate is like Hawaii's. Central and Northern Japan have snow in the winter. The typhoon season is in September, and the rainy season is in June.

Economy

Japan's economy has been close to being the world's strongest. In 1985 it led the world in television set production, was second in the production of cars, radios, and cement, and was third in steel production.

Only 20% of the land is arable, so much of its food is imported. Japan leads in fish production, is the fourth largest producer of eggs, and is the sixth largest grower of rice. Japan has the highest literacy rate in the world and the highest living standard in Asia, making for an excellent labor force. The Japanese person's thriftiness provides the banks with the funds to keep the economy running.

Transportation and Communication Systems

In Japan, mass transit is highly developed, efficient, and convenient. Consequently, only about 16% of the total population owns cars. Among the numerous newspapers and magazines, Tokyo has five English-language newspapers. Five commercial television networks and two public networks broadcast standard television fare. Dozens of radio stations thrive. The Japanese telephone system is fully automatic and perhaps the world's best. Mail service is prompt, with one-day delivery in some areas.

Health, Sanitation, and Medical Facilities

Japanese public health standards are not the best. Open drains carry sewage, and the water is not fluoridated. People are quite concerned about spreading disease and take great care not to do so, wearing surgical masks in public when suffering from a cold or the flu. Doctors and health facilities are excellent. Dentists and ophthalmologists are expensive, and most do not meet American standards.

Communication Style

Japanese communication is directed to one goal — harmony — which stems from religious influences. Achieving harmony requires minimizing differences, accepting incompatibilities, and emphasizing the aesthetic. Promoting harmony within each relationship calls for situational appropriateness. Each relationship has a defined role within the social hierarchy, requiring the citizens to acknowledge their status level and assume their proper place in the hierarchy. In the presence of their superiors, the Japanese display the behavior appropriate to their inferior status. When they are in a superior position, they take on the behaviors conforming to that role.

By following their prescribed situational roles, the Japanese find their identities not individually but instead through membership in the groups to which they belong. This group homogeneity or collectivisim encourages shared responsibility, togetherness, mutual solidarity, and reciprocal obligation, and it accentuates group welfare over individual needs. The Japanese refrain from expressing disagreement, acquiesce to group desires, and commit themselves totally to the group. In exchange for the individual's loyalty, the group looks after his or her welfare.

Through their long-term group memberships, the Japanese can acquire a vast amount of personal information about the group members. This accumulation of personal data allows for high-context communication to develop. As members of a high-context society, typical messages of the Japanese are implicit, in which the largest portion of the message either resides in the physical context or is internalized in the communicators. Verbiage is limited; not a lot of talk is necessary.

From the descriptive research reported in the multitude of sources about Japanese communication, a profile of the average Japanese communicator can be constructed. The Japanese speaker is honest, sincere, and authentic as an oral communicator. Speakers tend to be apprehensive in oral encounters, especially with strangers.

With a low inclination to verbalize, typical Japanese rely on nonverbal skills to communicate their feelings. Outwardly shy, the Japanese people tend to task-oriented talk and are at the same time submissive to authority. The talk reflects a deference to people of higher status. Generally calm and collected but not fluent, a typical Japanese person will be rated low as a friendly, attentive, contentious, animated, impression-leaving communicator, and a person who will not interact with those who are not of his or her group.

This description fits the stereotypical image of the Japanese as a silent and inscrutable people who place a high value on silence. In the Japanese view, people of a few words are thoughtful, trustworthy, and respectable. Speaking only modestly and sparingly, they depend upon the other person's sensitivity or sharp guesswork to decipher their needs and wants. Compared to many foreign cultures, people in the Japanese culture spend less time conversing and are apt to feel imposed upon by eloquent speakers. To the Japanese, speech is *a* means of communication not *the* means.

Useful Words and Phrases

Good morning: *Ohayo gozai mas*
Good afternoon: *Konnichiwa*
Good evening: *Kombanwa*
Goodbye: *Sayonara*
Mr., Mrs., or Miss Jones: *Jones san*
Good: *Yoroshii*
Bad: *Warui*
Yes: *Hai so desu*
No: *Iie*
What time? *Nanji desuka*

Thank you: *Arigato gozai mas*
Excuse me: *Gomen nasai*
I'm sorry: *Sumi masen*
Is that so? *So desuka*
One moment, please: *Chotto matte kudasai*
How much? *Ikura desuka*
I: *Watakushi*
You: *Anata*
How are you? *Ikaga desu ka*

Bibliography

Condon, J. C. *With Respect to the Japanese.* Yarmouth, MA: Intercultural Press, 1984.

Condon, J. C., and Saito, M. *Intercultural Encounters with Japan.* Tokyo: Simul Press, 1974.

Culturgrams: The Nations Around Us, Vol. 2. Provo, UT: Brigham Young University, 1986.

Japan, Hawthorn, Australia: Lonely Planet, 1997.

Japan Almanac, 1999, Tokyo: Asahi Shimbun, 1998.

Jensen, M. *Japan and Its World.* Princeton, NJ: Princeton University Press, 1980.

Kindaichi, H. *The Japanese Language.* Tokyo: Charles Tuttle, 1978.

Lanier, A. R. *Update: Japan.* Chicago: Intercultural Press, 1981.

Lebra, T. S. *Japanese Patterns of Behavior.* Honolulu: University Press of Hawaii, 1976.

Lebra, T. S., and Lebra, W. P. (Editors). *Japanese Culture and Behavior: Selected Readings.* Honolulu: University Press of Hawaii, 1974.

Maraini, F. *Meeting with Japan.* New York: Viking, 1959.

Meyer, M. W. *Japan: A Concise History.* Boston: Allyn and Bacon, 1966.

Nakane, C. *Japanese Society.* Los Angeles: University of California Press, 1970.

Nishiyama, K. Japan. *Occasional Papers in Speech.* Honolulu: University of Hawaii, 1975.

Storry, R. *Japan: Country of Today.* London: Ernest Benn Ltd., 1969.

Types of Intercultural Contact

Exercise 2 introduces you to the sorts of challenges that people can face when they come into intercultural contact. It also presents examples of the types of intercultural contact that people can have.

Objective

- To make you aware of the kinds of difficulties individuals might face in intercultural interactions

Reference

Factually based incidents drawn partially from *Intercultural Interactions: A Practical Guide*, by Brislin, Cushner, Cherrie and Yong (Beverly Hills, CA: Sage, 1986)

Instructions

1. Read each incident. Note that four possible explanations are listed under each incident.

2. Read the explanations for the first incident and make a judgment regarding each explanation. Place a "C" in the blank for the explanation you think is the correct one. Place an "L" in the blank for the explanation that to you seems a likely possibility but is not necessarily correct. Place a "U" in the blank for the explanation that is unlikely to be correct. Place an "N" in the blank for the explanation you feel sure is not correct.

3. Do the same for the other incidents.

4. Place your name in the space provided. Tear out and turn in on the date due.

5. Prepare to discuss the incidents in class. The correct answers will be announced.

Types of Intercultural Contact

1. **University Students Studying Overseas**

The departmental secretary for communication studies is well-liked and respected by students and faculty alike. She enjoys being of help to students who are working their way through departmental and university regulations. One day a student from India confronts her, demanding attention to problems he is having with his visa, low course grades, and master's degree thesis advisor. Speaking gruffly and like a superior talking to subordinates, he gives orders to the secretary without so much as a "please" or "thank you." The secretary tries to control her anger, finally going to the department chairperson to see if someone else can work with this student in the future. What do you think is the correct explanation for this incident?

_____ The Indian student was upset because no well-developed procedures had been developed for handling visa problems.

_____ The secretary was not being attacked personally; she was being confronted because of her role as secretary.

_____ The Indian was upset because he was getting low grades even though he was an excellent student.

_____ Foreign students occasionally are accused of plagiarizing others' work, and the Indian student believed he was so accused.

2. **Immigrants Working in the Host Country**

In the River Rouge plant of an American car maker, Jim works with several immigrants who are new arrivals to the United States. Jim enjoys their company and has made friends with them. A Samoan spends a lot of his free time with Jim and they drink together frequently. As far as Jim is concerned, though, the friendship is becoming strained because the Samoan borrows money from Jim regularly. The Samoan spends his wages long before the next payday arrives and then expects Jim to help him financially until payday. Jim thinks the Samoan should be more responsible and budget his money better. The Samoan laughs at Jim's suggestions about budgeting, saying, "Why worry? Good friends like you will help me out." Jim thinks the Samoan is being irresponsible and is taking advantage of Jim. What do you think is the correct explanation for the Samoan's attitude?

_____ Not having been brought up in a cash economy, the Samoan did not appreciate the value of money.

_____ The Samoan probably liked to drink, and he spent his money that way but wouldn't admit this to Jim.

_____ The Samoan way is to share possessions, including money.

_____ The Samoan had plans to leave for home soon, leaving his debts behind.

3. Students Attending Desegregated Schools

Kimo, a high school student from Hawaii, is sent to San Francisco on a special scholarship for advanced students. He is enrolled in a desegregated school as part of the scholarship program. A tall, handsome, and proud Hawaiian, he comes from a family with strong unity and deep pride in its Hawaiian heritage. This is Kimo's first trip away from home and from the Islands.

No other Hawaiians are attending the school, but several black girls take a liking to him and call him "brother." In subsequent weeks, Kimo's behavior becomes unsettled; he cuts class, tries to avoid the black students, and generally does poorly in his work. His aunt and uncle, with whom he lives, become aware of his behavior and send him back home to Honolulu. What do you think is the correct explanation for Kimo's behavior?

_____ Kimo resented going to San Francisco because of his attachment to his family.

_____ Kimo did not like the desegregated atmosphere in the school.

_____ Kimo was upset at being identified with a culture group other than his own.

_____ Hawaiian teenagers misbehave once they are away from home.

4. Student Tourists

American university students Lisa and Jane are on their first visit to southern Europe. Their first morning in Spain they discover a little cafe near the hotel with friendly service and good food. They have a pleasant breakfast inside the cafe. The next morning they return for breakfast. They decide to sit at one of the outdoor tables to enjoy the beautiful, warm morning. They have their breakfast and receive the bill only to discover that the cost has doubled for the same items they had the day before. They accuse the waiter of overcharging them. The waiter tries to explain in his inadequate English that they are sitting in a different place and must pay more. The two women don't believe the explanation, slam down the money, and storm out of the serving area, resentful for being exploited. What do you think is the correct explanation?

_____ They looked like suckers so the waiter "took" them.

_____ The waiter was stating a custom. Sitting outside costs more than sitting inside.

_____ They should refuse to pay and should call the police.

_____ These practices are common abroad, and the students should learn to accept them.

5. Students Studying in the United States

Ed, an outgoing, boisterous, talkative, but well-liked American, has a Thai roommate. They seem to get along well, and Ed is pleased because most of his former roommates did not like his company. About halfway through the semester, the Thai student announces that he is moving out. Ed is puzzled and asks the Thai student why. The Thai student is reticent about answering, but under Ed's persistent questioning he finally replies that Ed is too noisy, plays loud music, is untidy, and has visitors at all hours. Ed wants to know why he hasn't been told before of his seemingly disconcerting behavior. The Thai student refuses to answer. Which explanation do you believe is the correct one?

_____ He didn't want to anger Ed.

_____ He was overwhelmed by Ed's boisterous behavior.

_____ As a foreigner, he felt inferior to Ed and didn't think he should complain.

_____ He was not assertive enough to confront Ed directly.

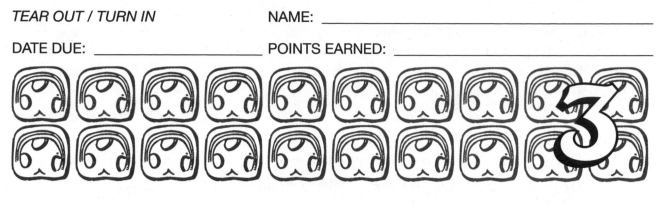

Cultural Communication Model

Exercise 3 reinforces what you have learned about interpersonal communication theory.

Objective

- To reconstruct and apply the interpersonal communication model

Instructions

1. Below is a sketch of an interpersonal communication model. Fill in the appropriate label for each component.

2. Consider the model as representing an intercultural situation — two people from different cultures speaking together. How would their talk likely differ?

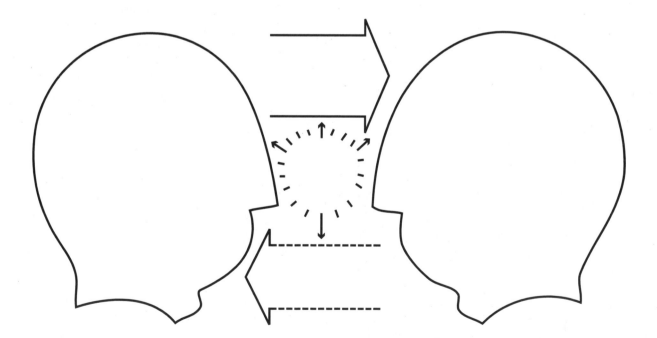

3. Read the statements below. Each pertains to some aspect of communication, its process, or the communicators. Circle the proper letter to indicate that you agree (A) or disagree (D) with each statement.

A   D   1.   Communication is a simple process.

A   D   2.   A person who is knowledgeable about a subject is highly likely to communicate it well.

A   D   3.   Extroverted people are much more likely than introverts to communicate well.

A   D   4.   The meaning of a word is seldom misunderstood.

A   D   5.   People who speak rarely have little to offer.

A   D   6.   If we state our points loudly and frequently, they will be accepted more readily.

A   D   7.   The one who is speaking is totally responsible for effective communication.

A   D   8.   An intelligent person is apt to understand a message the first time.

A   D   9.   A person with a large vocabulary will communicate more effectively.

A   D   10. Written communication is more effective than oral communication.

Name of country chosen for Exercise 1: _____.

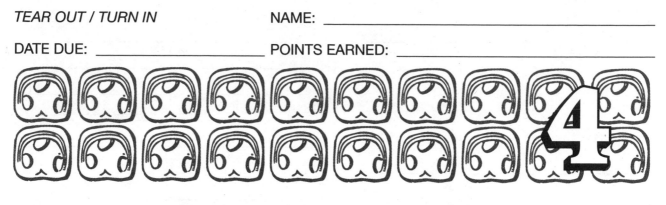

Cultural Universals

George Murdoch developed a list of cultural universals common to all cultures, past and present, with reference to what a culture's people both think and do.

Objective
- To apply Murdoch's cultural universals through examples

Reference
Chapter 2 of text

Instructions
1. Examine the list in the text. From it take 10 universals you think are interesting. Place those in the appropriate spaces below.
2. For each, list five examples drawn from your knowledge of the U.S. culture. For example, for the universal "athletic sports," you could name *football, baseball, basketball, track, softball.*

UNIVERSAL	EXAMPLES
1. _____	_____
	_____
	_____
	_____
	_____
2. _____	_____
	_____
	_____
	_____
	_____
3. _____	_____
	_____
	_____
	_____
	_____

4. _____

   _____

   _____

   _____

   _____

5. _____

   _____

   _____

   _____

   _____

6. _____

   _____

   _____

   _____

   _____

   _____

7. _____

   _____

   _____

   _____

   _____

8. _____

   _____

   _____

   _____

   _____

9. _____

   _____

   _____

   _____

   _____

10. _____

   _____

   _____

   _____

   _____

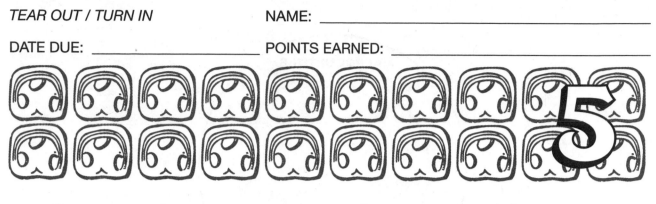

Becoming Aware of Yourself

The text describes the concept of microculture and names the subcultures as age, gender/sex, ethnic origin, religion, class, geographic region, urban/suburban/rural, and exceptionality.

In the example below, a 17-year-old student determined the importance of her membership in microcultures, all existing within the framework of her macroculture. Her gender/sex obviously is most important to her, as it represents the largest portion of the inner circle. Her religion follows in importance. The others play roles in her life but not to the extent of her interest in women's issues.

Objective

• To apply the concept of subcultures to yourself, a friend, and an acquaintance

Reference

Chapter 3 of text

Instructions

Using the circles on the reverse side, determine the importance of the microculture memberships you hold, those of a close friend, and those of an acquaintance, perhaps a fellow student. You will need to question the friend and the acquaintance about their memberships.

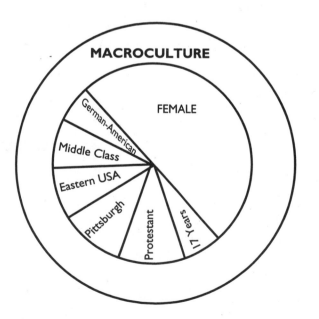

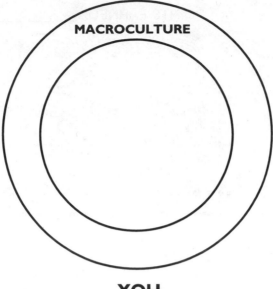

YOU

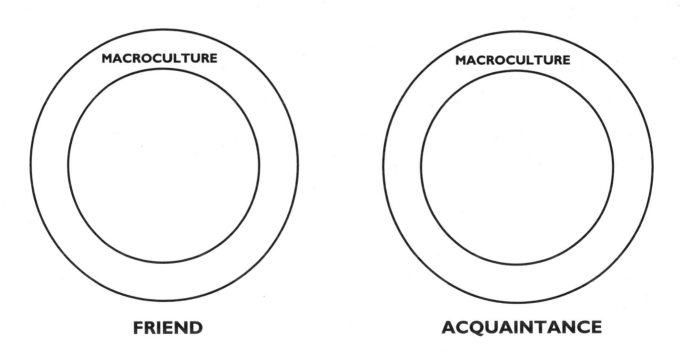

FRIEND

ACQUAINTANCE

What Does It Mean?

Check your knowledge of terms you learned in Part One in the text. Match the description with the correct word. Answers are on page 85.

_____ 1. Using the telephone, radio, newspapers.

_____ 2. Once a word is spoken, it cannot be taken back.

_____ 3. The process by which people share information, meanings, and feelings through the exchange of verbal and nonverbal messages.

_____ 4. Translating an already conceived idea into a message.

_____ 5. Boom!

_____ 6. People of equal status converse.

_____ 7. Translating a message into understandable meaning and feeling.

_____ 8. A set of rules for getting along in life.

_____ 9. Eat, drink, marry.

_____ 10. The dominant, universal culture.

a. Macroculture   b. Irreversible   c. Culture
d. Decoding   e. Human communication   f. Noise
g. Symmetrical   h. Mediated communication   i. Universals
j. Encoding

In the space below, write down 10 other terms defined and discussed in Part One of the text. Write an appropriate description for each.

1. _____   _____

2. _____   _____

3. _____   _____

4. _____   _____

5. _____   _____

6. _____   _____

7. _____   _____

8. _____   _____

9. _____   _____

10. _____   _____

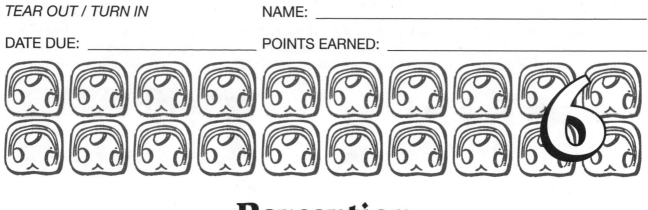

Perception

Our perception of people affects our communicative ability. Here, using traditional psychological methods, we illustrate some of the concepts related to perception.

Objective

- To apply the concepts of figure/ground, grouping, and closure.

Reference

Chapter 4 of text.

I. Figure and Ground

The process of perception involves three steps: selection, organization, and interpretation. Organization, our concern here, means to put the stimuli we select into a useful pattern that will make sense to us. One way of doing this is called *figure and ground*.

Instructions

1. What do you see in this drawing? Is it something black on a white ground? Or do white figures appear on a black ground? State your answer here.

2. Examine the two figures below. Do you see anything familiar or identifiable in either? Both have a message. In the left drawing the message is white on the partially black ground. In the drawing on the right, the message is black on a white background. What are the messages?

3. In Chapter 4, the discussion of figure and ground includes an example. It concerns blacks in all-white Europe during World War II. Can you now explain the meaning of this example in terms of the above drawings?

II. Grouping

Another way of organizing the stimuli we perceive is to group them according to proximity, similarity, and continuity. This concept is illustrated in this drawing:

```
 O O O O O      O O O O O
 O O O O O      O O O O O      O O O O O
 O O O O O      O O O O O      O O O O O
 O O O O O      O O O O O      O O O O O
 O O O O O      O O O O O      O O O O O
 O O O O O      O O O O O      O O O O O
       1            2              3
```

Objects (in the drawing — circles) or people who are close together tend to be grouped together. In the first grouping either horizontal rows or vertical columns can be seen with equal ease. In the second group the circles get closer together horizontally, and horizontal rows emerge. With the more vertical proximity of the third grouping, vertical columns appear.

Instructions

Relate this psychological phenomenon to the grouping of people. What happens when we perceive people of a given ethnic background, age, sex, education, occupation? Is this good or bad? Why?

3. Closure

The third way of organizing the stimuli we perceive is to make what we perceive into wholes. If a stimulus pattern is incomplete, we fill in the missing parts to make a whole. The drawings below illustrate this concept.

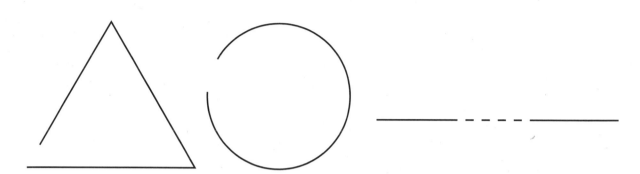

Parts are missing in the drawings, and our tendency is to complete or close the patterns the drawings represent. We make a triangle, circle, or straight line out of what we see.

If someone who is talking to us does not finish a sentence or thought, we are apt to complete the thought, aloud or in our head. We may err in the process, saying or thinking something the speaker may not have intended. Note what happens in these examples:

1. Sally: Gee! The weather...
   Mary: [. . . sure looks like it's going to be lousy. I'd better leave.]
   Sally: I hear it's going to be sunny all day.

2. Len: I think I'd better be leaving...
   Jim: [. . . Hurrah! His talk is driving me crazy!]
   Len: Yes, I should be leaving in another couple of hours, even though your hospitality is wonderful.

In the above examples, Mary and Jim silently complete the thoughts of Sally and Len. In doing so, they come up with inaccurate interpretations of what Sally and Len were going to say. Of course, we also can complete someone's incomplete message accurately.

Instructions

What might happen in a conversation with people representing another culture if we complete their incomplete statements? List some of the possible consequences.

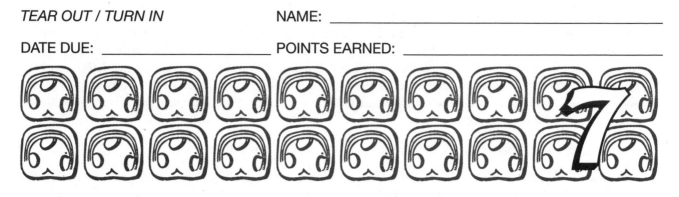

Disconfirmed Expectations/Attribution

This exercise deals with perceptual problems that sojourners often confront: disconfirmed expectations and attribution errors.

Objective

- To illustrate how misperceptions can cause misunderstandings, frustrations, and anxieties

Reference

Critical incidents in *Intercultural Interactions: A Practical Guide,* by Brislin, Cushner, Cherrie, and Yong (Beverly Hills, CA: Sage, 1986)

Instructions

1. Read each incident. Note that each offers four possible explanations for the behavior exhibited.

2. Place an "X" in the blank in front of the explanation you believe is most accurate for each.

I. Disconfirmed Expectations

1. Henry, a Nigerian, was accepted for graduate study in a large university in the United States. A member of a large extended family, his relatives were especially proud of this achievement because few Nigerians receive such an honor. After an orientation program, Henry began his coursework, taking graduate seminars with about 10 enrollees and required graduate classes with as many as 30 enrolled. Following the standard practice in the United States, the professors treated all students equally, giving extra attention after class to students who had questions. Henry soon believed his contributions were not being well received and the rest of the class did not give him sufficient attention for his efforts. After a few months, Henry's work fell off and he no longer enjoyed his classes. What do you think is the best reason for his loss of interest?

   _____ Henry was reacting to a loss in status.

   _____ Henry did not have sufficient orientation to university life.

   _____ Henry's Nigerian education did not prepare him well for study in the United States.

   _____ Henry's professors should have recognized Henry's problems and helped him out.

2. Peggy returned to school after a year's study in Paris, filled with new modes of doing things, which she wanted to use in her senior semester classes and in her sorority. Upon her arrival, she was greeted enthusiastically by her Gamma Chi Sigma sorority sisters. They overwhelmed her

with questions, then filled her in on all that had taken place during the past year. After the initial questions, they did not ask any more about her Paris experiences. The talk always was about local events, not about her trip. When someone did ask about Paris, Peggy noticed that no one paid much attention to her answers and the subject inevitably changed. After a few days of this, she became miserable and wished she had stayed in Paris. What do you think is an accurate assessment of Peggy's predicament?

_____ Peggy's sorority sisters really were not glad to have her back.

_____ Peggy was monopolizing conversations with her talk of Paris so the subject was changed to give others a chance.

_____ Peggy was tired from traveling and misinterpreted her friends' reactions.

_____ Peggy's expectations about returning were not being met, and culture shock was setting in.

II. Attribution Error

1. Beth had been teaching in an English language school in Tokyo for several years and was well-respected by her teaching colleagues. She was so highly thought of that the school managers often asked her to help train the new teachers. One new teacher was a Japanese national who spoke fluent English, and Beth worked with this new teacher, Hideto, for some time. Hideto was much concerned with several teaching practices and believed they could be improved. He was encouraged to develop his ideas into a new teaching plan. He did so, but the school's owner did not accept the plan because of the added expenses it entailed. When the school managers told him of the plan's rejection, Hideto said little. Later, at the local bar, where the teachers frequently met after class, Hideto criticized his superiors vigorously. Listening to his tirade, Beth concluded that Hideto was an aggressive Japanese male and that she would have difficulty continuing in her role as his mentor. Which of the following best explains Beth's conclusion?

   _____ From the behavior she observed, Beth was making an inappropriate judgment about Hideto's traits.

   _____ Beth believed that Hideto was attacking her personally.

   _____ In Japan, people's behavior in public is supposed to be highly proper, so Hideto's vigorous criticism makes him a difficult co-worker.

   _____ Because the school owner had failed to tell the faculty about creating new teaching schemes involving additional costs, Beth should be upset with the owner, not Hideto.

2. Alan Nanoy found foreign languages to his liking and took several applicable courses at the university. He always earned the highest grades and passed oral and written assignments with ease. Landing in Frankfurt, Alan thought he would use his excellent command of German and, at the cab stand, gave the driver directions to his hotel in German. The driver couldn't understand and pushed Alan out of the cab. After getting to the hotel with the help of an English-speaking cabbie, Alan went shopping, again speaking the German he had learned in college. The reactions were much like that of the cab driver. The store clerks didn't understand and treated him with disdain. Alan began to develop negative feelings about his German instructors and about Germany. What is the best analysis of Alan's feelings?

   _____ Alan should not have used the German language to communicate.

   _____ Alan was the target of prejudice, perhaps even jealousy.

   _____ Alan was overreacting to vivid, personal, but probably atypical events.

   _____ Foreign language instruction doesn't teach one how to speak the language very well.

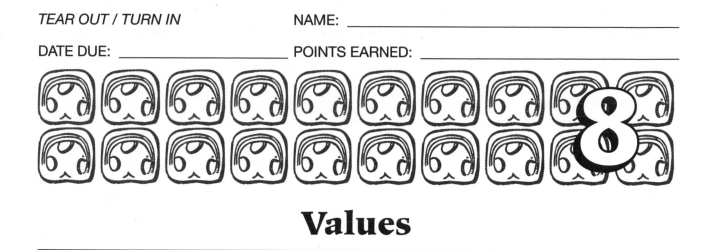

Values

Needs are the motivating factors in our personal orientation system. Values guide and direct the behavior that the needs activate. This exercise consists of three parts; each contains a value scale that you are to complete by following the instructions.

Objective

● To identify and clarify your values and determine which are most important

Reference

Chapter 5 in text

I: Value Word Scale

Instructions

1. Determine the importance of the 20 values in your life by checking the "primary" blank if you believe the value is primary in your life (most important and worth guarding at all costs), the "secondary" blank if you believe the value is of secondary importance (significant, but not significant enough to die for), the "tertiary" blank if you believe the value is third-ranked in importance (good to have but not worth getting bothered about), and the "not important" blank if you believe the value is insignificant in your life.

VALUE WORD	PRIMARY	SECONDARY	TERTIARY	NOT IMPORTANT
Individuality	_____	_____	_____	_____
Freedom	_____	_____	_____	_____
Equality	_____	_____	_____	_____
Democracy	_____	_____	_____	_____
Humanitarianism	_____	_____	_____	_____
Progress	_____	_____	_____	_____
Collectivism	_____	_____	_____	_____
Achievement	_____	_____	_____	_____
Activism	_____	_____	_____	_____
Practicality	_____	_____	_____	_____
Time	_____	_____	_____	_____
Informality	_____	_____	_____	_____

VALUE WORD	PRIMARY	SECONDARY	TERTIARY	NOT IMPORTANT
Morality	_____	_____	_____	_____
Respect for elders	_____	_____	_____	_____
Respect for parents	_____	_____	_____	_____
Respect for ancestors	_____	_____	_____	_____
Honesty	_____	_____	_____	_____
Emotional display	_____	_____	_____	_____
Work	_____	_____	_____	_____
Well-being of others	_____	_____	_____	_____

II: Value Questionnaire

Instructions

This questionnaire offers 10 dilemma-posing situations. Each situation gives three behavior alternatives. Choose the alternative you consider most appropriate for the circumstances.

1. In shark-infested waters, three men are adrift on a slowly sinking life raft. Their combined weight is too much to keep the raft afloat. Each weighs about 175 pounds. If one jumps off, the raft will float and the remaining two will survive. One is a 16-year old honor student, the second is a 45-year-old nuclear physicist, and the third is a 70-year old Nobel prize winner. Who should jump?

   _____ 16-year old

   _____ 45-year old

   _____ 70-year old

2. Even though the applicant scored high on the university entrance examinations, he was not admitted. The boy's parents heard that a courtesy payment to the school admission officer usually results in admission. What should the parents do?

   _____ Give money to the admission officer.

   _____ Meet with the admission officer but give her nothing.

   _____ Accept the school's decision not to enroll their son.

3. During the funeral of a family member, the relatives outwardly expressed their sorrow with much loud moaning and crying, hysterical emotion, and weeping. How would you respond at the funeral of a loved one?

   _____ Outwardly express your sorrow.

   _____ Show emotional restraint.

   _____ Repress all emotional displays.

4. A mother of two boys is confronted by the youngest son. He says, "You favor my brother over me. You should treat us as equals. I'm just as good as he is." The mother replies, "He's older than you." What do you think?

   _____ The mother should treat the boys as equals.

   _____ The mother should favor the older son.

   _____ The mother should favor the younger son.

5. Walking along the street, you see a person lying in the gutter. Dirty and ill-kempt, the person does not appear healthy. What would you do?

_____ Ignore the person.

_____ Ask him if he needs help.

_____ Give the help he requires.

6. The workday ends, and you are ready to quit work and have some fun. You need company. Whom do you ask to join you?

_____ Your co-workers.

_____ Your co-workers and selected friends.

_____ Your special friends.

7. You have 2 hours to prepare for an examination and a report you and several other students have to give. The report earns a group grade; the exam score is your own. In the 2 hours you can do only one assignment well. What would you do?

_____ Study for the test, not the group report.

_____ Prepare for the group report, not the test.

_____ Try to do both.

8. Poverty-stricken, you make only $100 per week, hardly enough to take care of your sick wife and disabled child. Walking along the street, you find $5,000 in an envelope with a name on it. What would you do?

_____ Return the money.

_____ Use the money for your wife and child.

_____ Keep the money and don't tell your wife and child.

9. Susan's parents are spending the weekend visiting relatives in a distant city. Susan is told to keep the house clean and hold no parties. Susan's friends pressure her to have a wild party. What should she do?

_____ Hold the party.

_____ Obey her parents.

_____ Compromise and have just a few friends over.

10. Your parents want you to attend a family reunion. Three friends you haven't seen for months call and want you to go out with them. They are in town for that day only. What would you do?

_____ Go with your parents.

_____ Go with your friends.

_____ Try to do both.

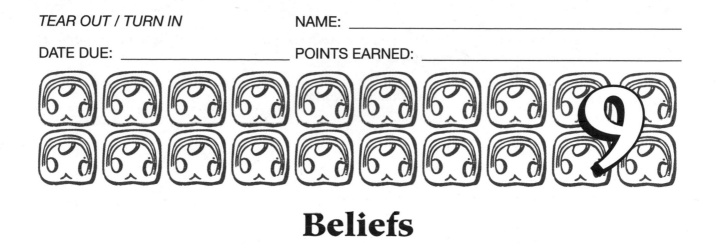

Beliefs

Worldview is a core of unchangeable beliefs. It is a cultural universal that has to be given high, if not first, priority in the study of a culture. Worldview permeates all aspects of a culture.

Objective

- To apply the concept of worldview to your own culture, then to the cultural resumé you are preparing, and finally, to compare the two worldviews

Reference

Chapter 5 of text

Instructions

1. Describe the worldview of your culture. Answers to these questions may help:
   - Does your culture believe in the existence of a Supreme Being?
   - Is the Supreme Being God?
   - Is the Supreme Being the ultimate controller of life and events, or do you as an individual exercise great control over your destiny?
   - Do the members of your culture try to dominate or control nature, or do they try to blend harmoniously with it or subordinate themselves to it?
   - Do the members of your culture compete against each other, placing their needs as individuals above those of other people, or do the members of your culture operate in a communal or cooperative manner, subordinating individual needs to those of the group?
   - What are the cultural beliefs regarding the origin of the people (e.g., Adam/Eve, evolution)?
   - What are your beliefs regarding the origin of people?
   - Does your culture believe in the supernatural?
   - If so, in what ways?
   - Does your culture believe that rocks, rivers, plants, thunderstorms, earthquakes, and every other form of inanimate reality have being?
   - Does your culture believe that certain individuals carry the power of curing, divining, serving as mediums with the spirit world?
   - Does your culture believe in some sort of afterlife (heaven or hell, for instance)?
   - Does your culture believe in reincarnation?

2. Examine the worldview of the culture you are studying for the Cultural Resumé required in Exercise 1. Summarize it in a paragraph or two.

Your Culture's Worldview

Worldview of Culture Studied

3. Compare the worldviews of your own culture and the one you are studying.

Worldview Comparison for the Two Cultures

Personal Attitude Profile

The results of this exercise are for your personal information only, so be honest in completing it.

Objective
● To examine your attitudes about cultural groups

Reference
Chapter 5 of text

Instructions
For each of the groups indicated below, check whether you feel favorably, unfavorably, neutral, or ignorant of the group because you never have had contact with a member of that group, have read nothing about the group, and are totally unaware of it.

GROUP	FAVORABLE	UNFAVORABLE	NEUTRAL	IGNORANT
1. American Indians				
2. Arabs				
3. Blacks				
4. Whites				
5. Canadians				
6. Chicanos				
7. Chinese				
8. French				
9. East Indians				
10. English				
11. Scandinavians				
12. Germans				
13. Italians				

GROUP	FAVORABLE	UNFAVORABLE	NEUTRAL	IGNORANT
14. Jews				
15. Irish				
16. Puerto Ricans				
17. Greeks				
18. Japanese				
19. Koreans				
20. Filipinos				
21. Spanish				
22. Turks				
23. Samoans				
24. Latin Americans				
25. Southerners				
26. Westerners				
27. Easterners				
28. Midwesterners				
29. Foreigners				
30. Africans				
31. Poor whites				
32. My neighbors				
33. My classmates				
34. My teachers				
35. My family				

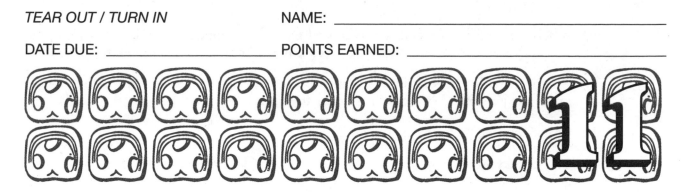

Stereotypes, Ethnocentrism, and Prejudice

Our classification of attitudes differentiates the negative manifestations of stereotypes, ethnocentrism, and prejudice. Most of the statements in this exercise reflect observations made by visitors to the United States and students from other countries.

Objective

• To understand the differences between stereotypical, ethnocentric, and prejudicial attitudes.

Reference

Chapter 6 of text

Instructions

For the statements below, identify the type of attitude by denoting "S" for stereotype, "E" for ethnocentrism, and "P" for prejudice.

_____ 1. Americans treat their elders with disdain, shipping off their elderly parents to "homes" to live out the years presumed to be their best.

_____ 2. Americans show hospitality to strangers but do not seem to care as much for family members.

_____ 3. Pollack, lesbo, queer, Hun, fag, Hebes, kooks.

_____ 4. Americans spend billions of dollars annually in tribute to foreign countries they want as their friends or that threaten them, yet their city streets are filled with bums, homeless people, and panhandlers.

_____ 5. The schools teach only the history of the United States because it's the only one that counts.

_____ 6. The Japanese have greater freedom of speech than Americans do.

_____ 7. To educate certain racial groups is a mistake because they may turn against the rest of us.

_____ 8. Americans acquiesce to the demands of small minorities — blacks for instance — because they are afraid of them.

_____ 9. Koreans are hot-tempered, aggressive, and stubborn.

_____ 10. Americans college students are interested only in the opposite sex, having fun, drinking, and sports. They don't care that their parents sacrifice to send them to school.

_____ 11. Americans call someone they just met a few days ago a "friend" when they hardly know the person. They seem to use their friends for their own gain.

_____ 12. Chinks are the "Jews of the Orient."

_____ 13. The United States may not be perfect, but it's as close to perfection as a country can get.

_____ 14. The United States isn't a democracy; it's run by special-interest groups and politicians who cater to those groups.

_____ 15. Blacks can't make a go of their stores because Korean grocers have taken over.

_____ 16. Buddhists, Hindus, and Confucianists are infidels; Christianity is God's religion.

_____ 17. American education is run by unions, not the teachers or parents. That's why the students can't read and write.

_____ 18. Jews take care of only their own group.

_____ 19. American Indians, blacks, and Hawaiians are looking for a free ride paid for by the rest of us. Most haven't earned the right to get on the bus.

_____ 20. He's so dumb he thinks a mini-skirt is what Mickey Mouse gave Minnie.

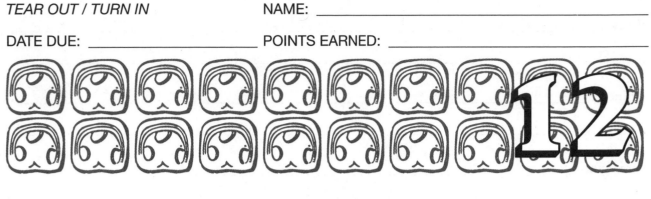

Stereotypes

One type of attitude is the stereotype, a fixed impression of a group of people that we apply to individual members of the group.

Objective

● To apply stereotypes to various cultures and thereby further understanding of the concept

Reference

Chapter 6 of text

Instructions

For each of the groups below, write down the adjectives that best represent to you the people making up the groups. For the North American group, some already are given as examples. Add to it as you wish.

American: [examples: outgoing, friendly, informal, loud, boastful, immature, hard-working, extravagant, wasteful, racially prejudiced, generous] _____

_____

British: _____

_____

Irish: _____

_____

German: _____

_____

Japanese: _____

_____

Black: _____

_____

Chinese: _____

_____

Mexican: _____

_____

Russian: _____

_____

Korean: _____

_____

Israeli: _____

_____

The culture being studied for Exercise 1 (if not listed above): _____

_____

? What Does It Mean?

The terms in this exercise come from Part Two in the text. Mark the following as either "T" for true or "F" for false. The answers are on page 85.

_____ 1. "Be all you can be" is *self-actualization*.

_____ 2. *Disconfirmed expectations* means that we anticipate something to happen in a certain way.

_____ 3. *Motivators* are influences that account for the initiation, direction, intensity, and persistence of behavior.

_____ 4. *Attribution* means to seek causes for behavior.

_____ 5. *Stereotyping* or indiscrimination means failure to discriminate.

_____ 6. Seeing and hearing are the major *distance* senses.

_____ 7. *Instincts* are innate, automatic dispositions to respond in a particular way to a specific stimuli.

_____ 8. *Perception* is the process by which individuals select, organize, and interpret sensory stimuli into a meaningless and incoherent picture of the world.

_____ 9. *Acquisition* means to surrender, comply, accept.

_____ 10. *Incentive* means there is something in it for us.

Match each statement with its proper meaning. The answers are on page 85.

_____ 1. Latest impressions.

_____ 2. We believe that because something happened, something else will occur.

_____ 3. Derived from personal experience.

_____ 4. Well-being of humankind.

_____ 5. Independent, responsible individuals seeking their own destinies.

_____ 6. The standards that guide our behavior.

_____ 7. Third order of importance.

_____ 8. Judgments about what is true or probable.

_____ 9. Caused by something beyond our control.

_____ 10. Physical and psychological feelings that give rise to tensions and hence motivate us in such a way as to overcome the tensions.

a. Values
b. Tertiary
c. Beliefs
d. Experiential
e. Reasoning
f. Individuality
g. Needs
h. Recency
i. Humanitarianism
j. External locus of control

Social Institutions

This exercise calls for you to examine the effect of social institutions on your life. Some of the information requested is personal; therefore, you do not have to turn in this exercise.

Objective

To give you a better understanding of your relationships with others

Reference

Chapter 7 of text

Instructions

Complete the following questions.

1. **Your family name.** What is it? Where does it come from? What does it mean? [Example: My name is Oxford. It is an English name. It was given to families that lived in close proximity to an English-river crossing for oxen.]

   _____

   _____

   _____

   _____

2. **Your family.**

   Type: Nuclear _____   Extended _____

   Structure: Monogamous _____   Polygamous _____   Patriarchal _____   Matriarchal _____

   Parents' mate selection: They decided _____   Marriage arranged _____

   Ethnic background: _____

   Religious faith: _____

   Political party affiliation: _____

3. **Your parents' work.**

   Father's occupation: _____

   Mother's occupation: _____

4. **Your schooling.**

   Type: Public _____ Private _____ Church-affiliated _____

   Year in college: _____

   Major: _____

   Learning style in high school: In-context _____ Out-of-context _____

   Classroom interaction style (check text for different styles):

   _____

5. **Your voluntary association memberships.** List the ones you now hold:

   _____

   _____

6. **Your interpersonal relationships.** List the types of relationships you have with other people, and indicate the status you hold in each (superior, subordinate, or equal):

   _____

   _____

   _____

   _____

   _____

   _____

7. **Your roles in life.** List the roles you assume in your interpersonal interactions.

   _____

   _____

   _____

   _____

   _____

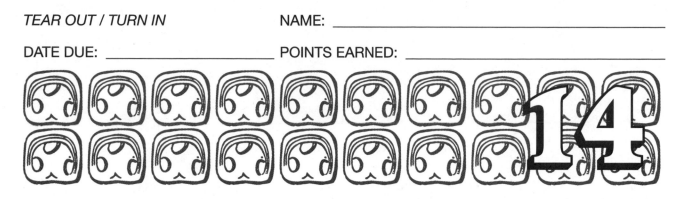

Social Institutions of Your Cultural Resumé

Objective
To analyze the social institutions of your cultural resumé

Reference
Chapter 7 of text

Instructions
For the culture you are studying, provide the following information regarding its institutions:

Name of culture/country: _____

Type of family unit: _____

Basic family structure: _____

Marital affiliation: _____

Educational system: _____

_____

Religion(s): _____

_____

Political system/Type of government: _____

_____

Economic system: _____

_____

Briefly summarize its history: _____

_____

_____

_____

_____

_____

_____

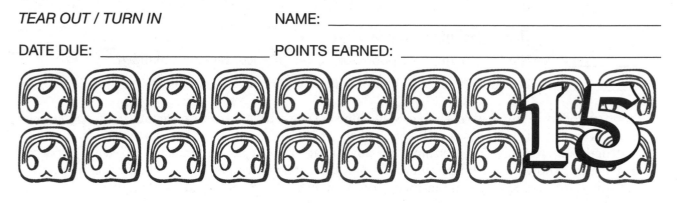

Interpersonal/Intercultural Relationships

These five incidents concern interpersonal relationships that are intercultural in nature. From the knowledge you have gained thus far, you are asked to provide a solution.

Objective

• To apply your understanding of intercultural relationships to hypothetical incidents

Reference

Chapter 8 of text

Instructions

For each incident, four alternatives are given. One offers the best explanation to the problem posed in the incident. Check the one you think is the best. Explanations are on page 51.

1. Mrs. Mordeno came to Honolulu to visit her son, José, who operated an art gallery there. He married one of his clients, Beth, who paints in her own studio near his gallery. Mrs. Mordeno's trip was her first out of the Philippines, and she wanted to see all of the scenic spots in the islands. José and Beth were expected to accompany her at the expense of their own work schedules. Mrs. Mordeno planned to stay only a week but enjoyed herself so much that she decided to stay another month. She wanted to invite her sister and her sister's children to stay with her. José's apartment was small and didn't have enough room for all of them, and José was expected to pay the travel expenses for all. He tried to explain the situation to his mother. She seemed to accept his tactfully presented arguments and seemed to be satisfied for a few days. Then one day she packed up and returned home.

   In your estimation, why did Mrs. Mordeno leave?

   _____ a. Mrs. Mordeno had other plans and just changed her mind.

   _____ b. José's inhospitality hurt her, and she considered him disrespectful.

   _____ c. She felt guilty for imposing on José and Beth.

   _____ d. Unable to deal with the pressures of Honolulu, she decided to leave.

2. In Amman, an American supervisor was discussing a draft of a report with his Jordanian employee. He requested that more than half of it be rewritten, suggesting that the Jordanian had misunderstood him. The Jordanian was deeply disturbed and wondered why the American didn't like him.

   What is your estimation of the situation?

   _____ a. The American didn't like the Jordanian.

_____ b. The Jordanian was too sensitive.

_____ c. The Jordanian was a poor worker who needed to be reprimanded.

_____ d. The American could have handled the matter more tactfully.

3. Yoko enrolled in an eastern United States university to begin work on her master's degree. Her flight from Japan was uneventful, yet she had jet-lag and her apartment was unsatisfactory. Her instructors were nice, however, and her advisor arranged a new apartment for her. One of the instructors, known to be hospitable to foreign students, invited her to a football game on her first Saturday in town. She agreed but then failed to appear at the appointed meeting place.

Why do you think Yoko failed to keep the appointment?

_____ a. She thought the instructor was a wolf who wanted to take advantage of her.

_____ b. She forgot the date and time.

_____ c. She was tired and had too much to do in her new apartment.

_____ d. She agreed to go because she didn't want to turn down a person of higher status, although she really didn't want to go.

4. Bud, in Frankfurt on business, was invited to dinner by his German business associate. For Bud, the cocktail hour begins when the flag is lowered in the late afternoon. That was the time he arrived at the German's house. No sooner had he arrived than he was ushered into the dining room for dinner. A glass of wine accompanied the meal. Smoking, Bud's favorite pastime, seemed forbidden. After dinner Bud excused himself and went back to his hotel.

Bud's dinner host, a good friend, certainly knew of Bud's need for drink and to smoke. Why did he not accommodate Bud?

_____ a. Europeans think hard liquor and smoking both dull the taste buds and prevent the enjoyment of fine food.

_____ b. The German business associate was a teetotaler.

_____ c. As a guest, Bud failed to bring the spirits.

_____ d. Bud obviously upset the host and hostess, and they reciprocated by failing to meet his needs.

5. Pauline, a Polish high school exchange student in the United States, was amazed at the way American teenagers spent their time. When classes were finished by two o'clock, she headed for the local pizza parlor with her American friends and fooled around there for several hours or went to the local mall to hang out. Then she went to the home of her hosts and watched television until her hosts came home from work. After a quickly prepared meal, she watched more TV. She had little homework, and what she had to do was easy and readily completed. She said of her American educational experience, "It is not a good thing to get used to."

Why do you think she felt as she did?

_____ a. She didn't like pizza and quick meals.

_____ b. American television is too violent for her.

_____ c. She had trouble with English.

_____ d. Her Polish education was much more demanding, and she was not used to all the free time.

INTERPERSONAL RELATIONS
EXPLANATION FOR THE ALTERNATIVES

1. Mrs. Mordeno flies back to the Philippines.

   a. The first alternative seems unlikely as Mrs. Mordeno was prepared to stay another month.

   b. Mrs. Mordeno expected the full attention of her son and his wife, as Filipinos would do back home. Furthermore, his rejection of her sister's family was a rejection of her, and an indication of his ingratitude. This is the best explanation.

   c. This answer is not in keeping with the Filipino tradition. José would be expected to do his best to please her.

   d. Perhaps Mrs. Mordeno was unable to handle the pressures of Honolulu, but they certainly are not as great as she experiences in Manila. The incident did not offer clues about any pressures. This is an unlikely answer.

2. The Jordanian and the American supervisor.

   a. No evidence is given to suggest dislike. It is an incorrect choice.

   b. This illustrates a cultural difference, not a flaw. Arabs believe that evaluation of their work, if stated too bluntly, is a personal insult.

   c. This is an unsubstantiated choice. No evidence supports that the Jordanian was a poor worker.

   d. This is the best answer. The American should be attuned to Arab feelings about evaluation. As a supervisor, he ought to know what constitutes proper evaluation. Complimenting the Jordanian on his work would help, as would a remark such as, "A few things should be revised in your draft. Let's work through them together."

3. The football game invitation.

   a. No evidence suggests that the instructor was perceived as anything but helpful. This is an unlikely explanation.

   b. Japanese people usually are dependable and keep their appointments. This alternative is unlikely.

   c. This is a possibility. The football game would have taken only a couple of hours, though, and Yoko could have scheduled her time accordingly.

   d. This is the best answer, yet it does not account for her rudeness in not showing up. She should have excused herself earlier.

4. Bud's thirst.

   a. This is the correct answer. The cocktail hour before a meal is short, if it exists at all, and there is no smoking during meals. If Bud had remained, he would have had all he wanted to drink and he could have smoked to his heart's content. After coffee, drink would have flowed.

   b. No evidence supports the contention that the businessman did not drink.

   c. Although guests should bring a gift when invited for dinner in Germany, supplying the spirits is not expected. A box of candy or flowers would be appropriate.

   d. No evidence supports the contention that Bud had upset the host and hostess.

5. Pauline's American education.

   a. No evidence suggests that Pauline didn't like pizza or quick meals.

   b. No evidence supports the contention that Pauline didn't like TV violence.

   c. Speaking a foreign language could have been a problem for Pauline, but nothing in the incident suggests that her language capability affected her thinking about American education.

   d. Polish education, like most European educational systems, is intense. In Warsaw, where Pauline lives, students are in class until late afternoon. When they arrive home, they eat and then they do their homework for four or five more hours before retiring. American education seemed tame to Pauline. This is the correct answer.

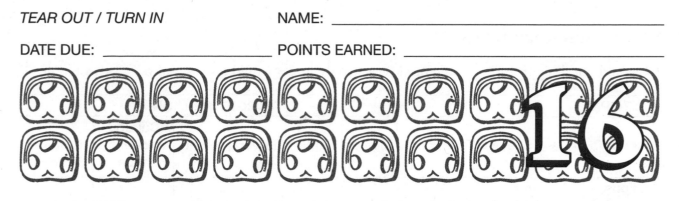

Self Disclosure in Intercultural Relationships

How much of yourself do you disclose to people? What innermost thoughts and feelings do you reveal, to what extent, and to whom? This exercise asks you to examine what you would disclose to potential communicative partners. The partners are Mother, Father, Lover, Friend, Acquaintance from the culture you are studying, and Stranger from that culture. The exercise asks you to identify the topics about which you would self-disclose and to what level of self-disclosure you would reach with each. The levels are:

    0 = would not disclose any of my thoughts or feelings on this topic
    1 = would talk in general terms about this topic
    2 = would disclose fully on this topic
    3 = would lie or misrepresent my thoughts or feelings on this topic

Objective

- To investigate our own feelings regarding self-disclosure, including self-disclosure to people from cultures different from our own.

Reference

Chapter 7 of text

Instructions

On the Self-Disclosure Scale, place the appropriate symbol in the space provided for each topic and for each partner.

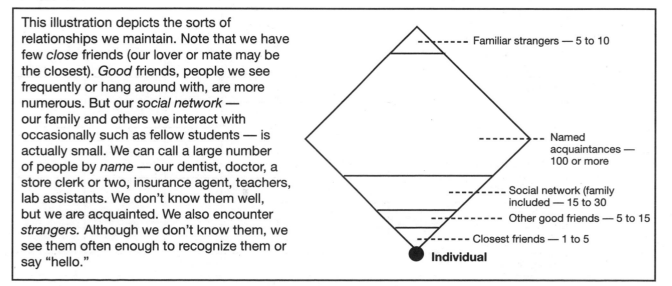

This illustration depicts the sorts of relationships we maintain. Note that we have few *close* friends (our lover or mate may be the closest). *Good* friends, people we see frequently or hang around with, are more numerous. But our *social network* — our family and others we interact with occasionally such as fellow students — is actually small. We can call a large number of people by *name* — our dentist, doctor, a store clerk or two, insurance agent, teachers, lab assistants. We don't know them well, but we are acquainted. We also encounter *strangers.* Although we don't know them, we see them often enough to recognize them or say "hello."

Familiar strangers — 5 to 10

Named acquaintances — 100 or more

Social network (family included — 15 to 30

Other good friends — 5 to 15

Closest friends — 1 to 5

Individual

Self-Disclosure Scale

0 = would not disclose   1 = would disclose generally   2 = would disclose fully   3 = would lie

TOPIC		TARGET PERSON					
General Area	Specific Topic	Mother	Father	Lover	Friend	Cultural Acquaintance	Cultural Stranger
Opinions	Religion						
	Communism						
	Race integration						
	Sex standards						
	Social standards						
Interests and Tastes	Food						
	Music						
	Reading						
	TV and movies						
	Parties and socials						
Work or Studies	Disabilities						
	Assets						
	Ambitions						
	Career choice						
	Co-workers/students						
Financial	Income						
	Debts						
	Savings						
	Needs						
	Budget						
Personality	Disability						
	Self-control						
	Sex life						
	Guilt/shame						
	Pride						
Body	Satisfaction with face						
	Ideal appearance						
	Body adequacy						
	Illnesses						
	Sexual adequacy						

The terms in the following exercises come from Part Two in the text. The answers are on page 85.

I. True (T) or False (F)

_____ 1. The *nuclear family* consists of the father, mother, and children plus aunts, uncles, and grandparents.

_____ 2. *Incest taboo* is the name for the newest perfume for Egyptian men.

_____ 3. *Monogamy* is forbidden in Alaska and the Hawaiian Islands.

_____ 4. *Polygyny* is the most popular form of <u>polygamy</u>.

_____ 5. In *polyandry* brothers typically share a wife.

_____ 6. *Exogamy* is the process of dying, according to existentialists.

_____ 7. *Endogamy* means to end it all.

_____ 8. The *patriarchal family* is prized because it is the most patriotic.

_____ 9. The *matriarchal family* is ruled by the father or oldest man.

_____ 10. In industrial societies, the *state* assumes some family functions.

II. Match each term with the appropriate statement.

_____ 1. Common in preliterate cultures.

_____ 2. Likes to learn with others.

_____ 3. Learns in the field.

_____ 4. The old teach the young.

_____ 5. Prefers to learn alone.

_____ 6. Classroom learning.

_____ 7. The young teach the old.

_____ 8. Recognizes ways other than our own.

_____ 9. Learns in environment different from where it is applied.

_____ 10. Peers teach peers.

a. Cofigurative
b. Global perspective
c. Field-sensitive
d. In-context
e. Informal education
f. Field-independent
g. Out-of-context
h. Formal
i. Prefigurative
j. Postfigurative

III. Match the term with its appropriate description.

_____ 1. Money is sweet potatoes.

_____ 2. One god.

_____ 3. MORE.

_____ 4. Cartels are formed to control prices.

_____ 5. Afterlife.

_____ 6. Social and physical world is inhabited by spirits.

_____ 7. Worldly and secular.

_____ 8. Countries are ruled by a strongman or small elite.

_____ 9. A timeless, external force greater than humans and nature.

_____ 10. Ability to determine the behavior of others.

a. Power
b. Anglo-American system
c. Monotheism
d. Authoritarianism
e. Abstract
f. Profane
g. Po
h. Papua
i. Asian system
j. Animism

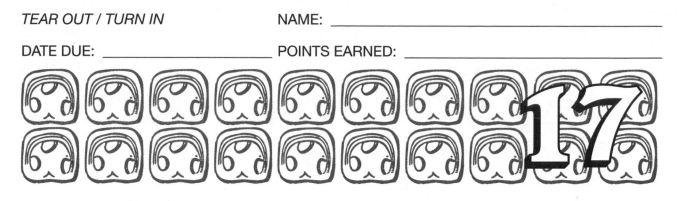

Language and Communication

Objective

● To apply the concept of language to a specific culture

Reference

Chapter 9 of text

Instructions

In several paragraphs describe the language of the culture you are studying for Exercise 1. Make the description simple and to the point. In your description, cover pronunciation, grammar, style, and writing system, at least. Here is a sample using the Japanese.

> In some respects, the Japanese language is considered difficult to learn, especially its writing system; in other respects, especially in its pronunciation, it is easy.
>
> Traditionally, Japanese has been written vertically, beginning at the top, right side and moving down the page. Horizontal writing also is used, written in the manner of English. Books and newspapers open from left to right.
>
> Japanese belongs to the SOV (Subject-Object-Verb) class of languages, but the subject and the object can be interchanged without altering the meaning. For example: *Mary-wa* (subject) *John-o* (object) *aisu* (verb) also can be *John-o Mary-wa aisu*. The meaning in both cases is the same — *Mary loves John*. The *wa* and *o* identify which is the subject and which is the object.
>
> To show interrogation, the participle *ka* is added to the end of the sentence. All modifiers precede the modified word. Different styles of speaking are used depending upon the person to whom one is speaking. The higher the status, the more formal is the language.
>
> Japanese uses three different systems of writing.
>
> 1. *Kanji* (Chinese characters), imported about the Third Century, are derived from stylized pictures of objects. About 2,000 of the 60,000 kanji are used in ordinary writing.
>
> 2. *Hiragana* is one of two Japanese syllabic characters, and it has a cursive flowing style. It is used most often with kanji.
>
> 3. *Katakana* is another syllabic alphabet, used mostly to spell out foreign words.

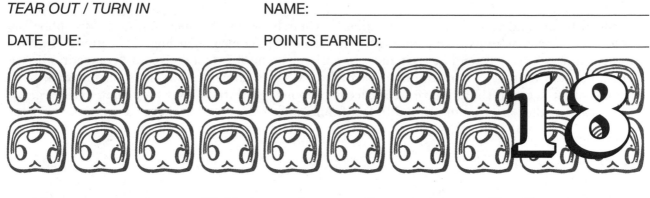

Language Meaning Across Cultures

Objective

- To explore the differences in meaning derived by different people in the same culture and across cultures

I. Meanings Within Cultures

Intercultural communicators must overcome "egocentric bias" when speaking to someone of another culture. This bias involves the assumption that if we say something that makes good sense to us, it should make sense to everyone else. This notion is about as unrealistic as it is widespread.

We tend to believe that if we don't know what a word or phrase means, all we have to do is use the dictionary for help. Unfortunately, dictionaries do not convey the entire subjective reaction that a word or phrase elicits. The dictionary meaning is based on conventional and formal rules of use; it doesn't get at the psychological meaning attached to words. Dictionaries do not deal with the interests, perceptions, beliefs, and attitudes culturally attached to words.

To illustrate that words have different psychological meanings, look at the word "education" from the frame of reference of a priest and a football coach, two individuals from the same culture. They picture a set of meanings similar to those shown in this graph.

The unshaded portion represents the priest's interpretation of "education" and the shaded portion, the coach's. The length of each portion indicates the significance each person attaches to the meanings. Thus, for the priest, "education," carries four possible meanings. "Morality" and "school"

Meanings	Mentioned	Important	Very Important	Crucial
Morality				
School				
Church				
Physical fitness				
Discipline				
Sports				
Competition				

☐ PRIEST   ■ COACH

are crucial to an understanding of "education." "Church" is most important, and "discipline" is mentionable. The coach obviously has a different frame of reference regarding "education." To him, "physical fitness" and "discipline" are most important, "school," "sports," and "competition" are important, and "morality" is mentionable. Based on what is known about their occupations, both the priest and the coach should have strong feelings about "education." Yet they don't agree regarding its meaning; they are coming from different frames of reference within the same culture.

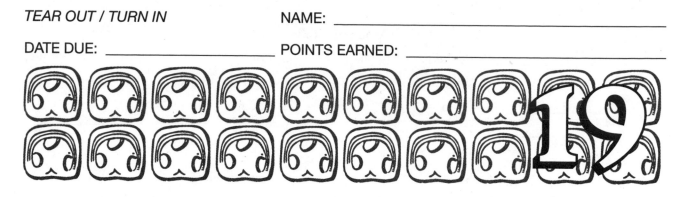

Subculture/Culture Argots/Dialects/Languages

Each subculture has its own unique language use — its argot, the specialized vocabulary and idioms of those who share a way of life. Argots are keys to attitudes, to modes of thinking, to evaluations of persons and society, to social organization, and to technology of a group of people. In this exercise you will examine the argots of specific subcultures to illustrate what argots are like. Brief lexicons are presented for each of the four subcultures, and they are presented as matching quizzes.

Objective

• To gain insight into a culture through its use of verbal language

Reference

Chapter 9 of text

Instructions

Match the righthand column, consisting of general-language terms, with the corresponding subculture language terms in the left column. Place the appropriate letter from the right column next to its matching number in the left column.

Prostitute Talk

_____ 1. Trick	a. Lawyer
_____ 2. Steak	b. A $50 client
_____ 3. Champagne	c. Exaggerate
_____ 4. Nunnery	d. The madam
_____ 5. Mother Superior	e. Client
_____ 6. Yeasting	f. Prostitute thief
_____ 7. Ginger	g. Multiple orgy
_____ 8. Party	h. A $300 client
_____ 9. Oil	i. Bordello
_____ 10. Lip	j. Police payola

Mountain Talk

_____ 1. Peaked   a. Look

_____ 2. Askeered of   b. Heat up, upset

_____ 3. Doin's   c. Eaten

_____ 4. Dast   d. Breezy

_____ 5. Et   e. Pale

_____ 6. Shed of   f. Frightened

_____ 7. Kivver   g. Dare

_____ 8. Het   h. A function

_____ 9. Airish   i. Get rid of

_____ 10. Gander   j. Cover

Hawaii Dialect

_____ 1. Hana hau   a. Hors d'oeuvres

_____ 2. Keiki   b. Crazy

_____ 3. Kokua   c. Finished

_____ 4. Ohana   d. Caucasian

_____ 5. Pau   e. Family

_____ 6. Pupule   f. Again

_____ 7. Pupus   g. Child

_____ 8. Haole   h. Help

_____ 9. Zoris   i. Right on

_____ 10. Akamai   j. Footwear

Note: Argot is subject to constant change. Thus, the lexicon for the three subcultures noted here may have undergone alterations.

II. We can gain insight into a culture by examining its use of language. A few commonly used terms of three different languages are given next.

Instructions

Match each foreign language term with its English equivalent.

German

_____ 1. Bierstube   a. Excessive sentimentality

_____ 2. Blitzkrieg   b. Tavern (beer)

_____ 3. Erzatz   c. Comfortable, snug

_____ 4. Gasthaüs   d. Out of order, broken

_____ 5. Gemutlich   e. Lightning attack

_____ 6. Gesundheit   f. Inferior substitute

_____ 7. Herrenvolk   g. Inn, hotel

_____ 8. Kaput   h. Bless you!

_____ 9. Luftwaffe   i. Air Force

_____ 10. Schmalz   j. Master race

Islamic

_____ 1. Allah   a. Holy month

_____ 2. Ayatollah   b. Ruler, governor, judge

_____ 3. Dervish   c. Shiite religious leader

_____ 4. Hakim   d. Scholar or teacher of holy law

_____ 5. Houri   e. Muslim sacred book

_____ 6. Jihad   f. Person who does whirling dances

_____ 7. Koran   g. God, Supreme Being

_____ 8. Mosque   h. Nymph or virgin

_____ 9. Mullah   i. Holy war

_____ 10. Ramadan   j. House of worship

Spanish

_____ 1. Bodega   a. Afternoon nap or rest

_____ 2. Caballero   b. Wineshop

_____ 3. Cantina   c. Tomorrow, shortly

_____ 4. Fiesta   d. Holiday

_____ 5. Hosteria   e. Gentleman

_____ 6. Mañana   f. Bar

_____ 7. Siesta   g. Restaurant

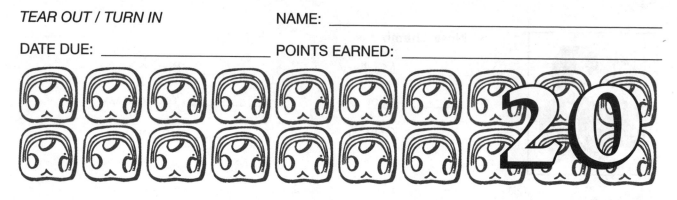

Nonverbal Communication: Gestures

Gestures, a form of nonverbal behavior, carry different meanings across cultures. This exercise is designed to show how meanings do vary from culture to culture.

Objective

• To point out the importance of nonverbal communication through common hand gestures

Reference

Chapter 10 of text

Instructions

Reproduced below are 10 commonly used gestures. Some are clear from the position of the hand. Others involve a characteristic movement that is difficult to duplicate in a drawing. A number of meanings have been stated for each gesture. Place a checkmark beside the one that best represents the meaning to you.

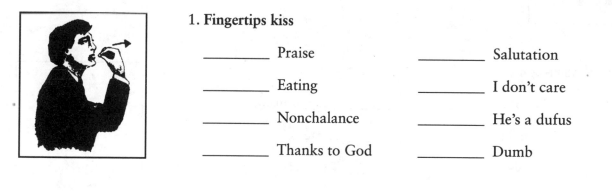

1. Fingertips kiss

_____ Praise		_____ Salutation
_____ Eating		_____ I don't care
_____ Nonchalance		_____ He's a dufus
_____ Thanks to God		_____ Dumb

2. Fingers Cross

_____ Protection	_____ Break friendship
_____ Okay — good	_____ Swear oath
_____ Friendship	_____ Copulation
_____ Go to toilet	_____ Calling a waiter

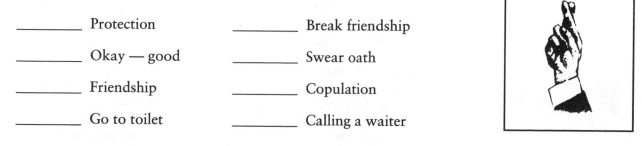

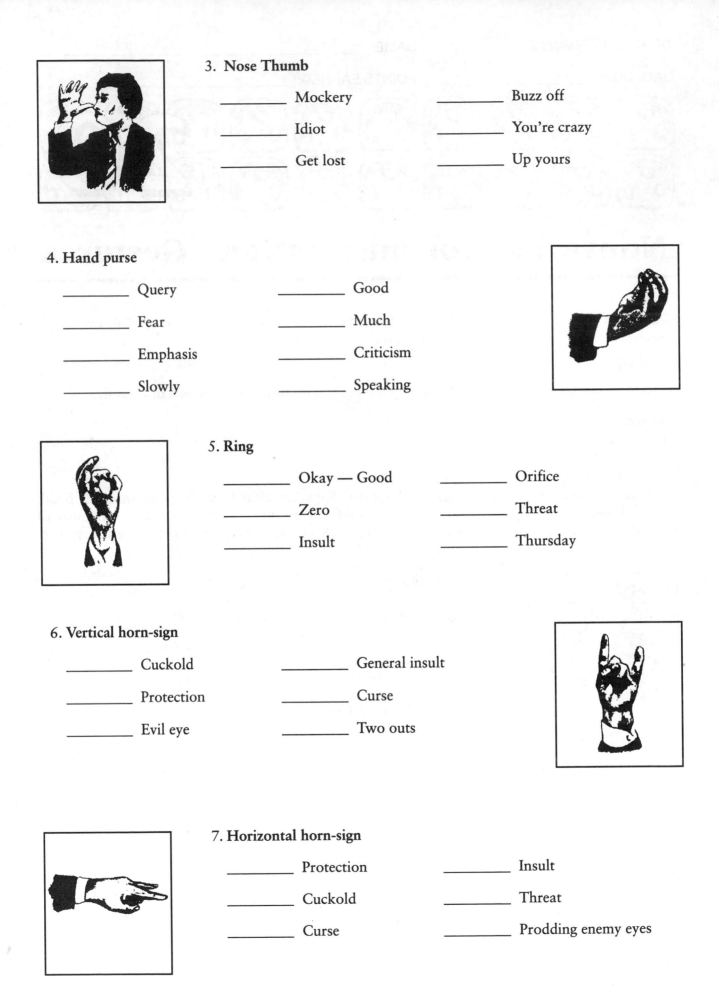

3. **Nose Thumb**

_____ Mockery   _____ Buzz off

_____ Idiot   _____ You're crazy

_____ Get lost   _____ Up yours

4. **Hand purse**

_____ Query   _____ Good

_____ Fear   _____ Much

_____ Emphasis   _____ Criticism

_____ Slowly   _____ Speaking

5. **Ring**

_____ Okay — Good   _____ Orifice

_____ Zero   _____ Threat

_____ Insult   _____ Thursday

6. **Vertical horn-sign**

_____ Cuckold   _____ General insult

_____ Protection   _____ Curse

_____ Evil eye   _____ Two outs

7. **Horizontal horn-sign**

_____ Protection   _____ Insult

_____ Cuckold   _____ Threat

_____ Curse   _____ Prodding enemy eyes

8. Thumb up

_____ Directional   _____ Hitchhike

_____ Okay   _____ One

_____ Sexual insult   _____ Obscenity

9. Palm-back V-sign

_____ Horns   _____ Two

_____ Victory   _____ Sexual insult

_____ Cuckold   _____ Eye poke

10. Forearm jerk

_____ Strength   _____ Up yours

_____ Boredom   _____ Effeminate

_____ Beckon   _____ Sexual insult

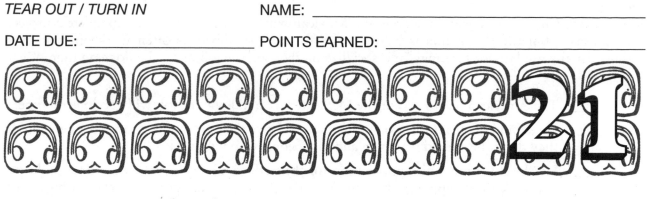

Nonverbal Communication: Time

The concept of time varies from culture to culture. This point is illustrated in the two sets of exercises that follow. The first sets forth critical incidents for you to analyze. The second asks you to differentiate monochronic and polychronic time.

Objective

- To illustrate concepts of time as demonstrated through nonverbal communication

I. Critical Incidents

Instructions

Read each incident, and choose the alternative you think is most accurate.

1. An American engineer has an appointment with Mr. Mahmoodi to visit and inspect a construction site in Tabriz, Iran, where a joint construction project is under way. The meeting, scheduled several weeks ago, is to take place just prior to the American's departure for home. As they are about to leave, Mr. Mahmoodi's brother shows up. What probably will happen?

   _____ Mahmoodi will ask his brother to accompany them.

   _____ Mahmoodi will ask his brother to wait for him at home.

   _____ Mahmoodi will postpone the trip to the site.

2. An American businessman visiting Tokyo has presented to a group of Japanese businessmen his plan for developing a business relationship. Several weeks have gone by and he is waiting for their answer. The Japanese have been hospitable, wining and dining the American in the evenings and filling his days with golf. Business is not brought up at these events. What is the reason for the Japanese actions?

   _____ They want to get to know the American better to determine whether he is genuine and trustworthy.

   _____ They are opposed to the plan but don't want to tell him that, so they are waiting for him to leave. They don't want to be poor hosts, however, so they are entertaining him.

   _____ They are circulating his proposal among all of the people affected by it, and this takes time. Meanwhile, they are trying to make his stay a pleasant one.

3. In Mexico City an American in charge of a Mexican work crew is expected to complete a project in 2 weeks, but the production is below the goals set. The Mexicans often work on their own time, usually are late for meetings, and socialize on the job. The job has to be done on time. What can he do?

_____ The American has to accept the Mexican pace and hope the job will get done on time.

_____ He should confront the worst offenders and give them one more chance to shape up. If they don't, he should fire them and hire people who will work.

_____ He should express his appreciation for their efforts to date, explain the time problem, and seek their support. Then he should enhance his own personal relationships with the workers.

II. Monochronic/Polychronic Time

Reference
Chapter 10 of text

Instructions
Identify each statement as adhering to monochronic ("M") or polychronic ("P").

_____ 1. Do many things at once.

_____ 2. Concentrate on the task at hand.

_____ 3. Adhere to time schedules.

_____ 4. Are low-context.

_____ 5. Are easily distracted.

_____ 6. Place a premium on promptness.

_____ 7. Alter plans readily.

_____ 8. Are committed to human relations.

_____ 9. Would not disturb a conversation.

_____ 10. Tend to be high-context.

_____ 11. Do one thing at a time.

_____ 12. See time commitments as a goal to reach, if possible.

_____ 13. Don't mind interruptions.

_____ 14. Are deadline-oriented.

_____ 15. Believe that people come before schedules.

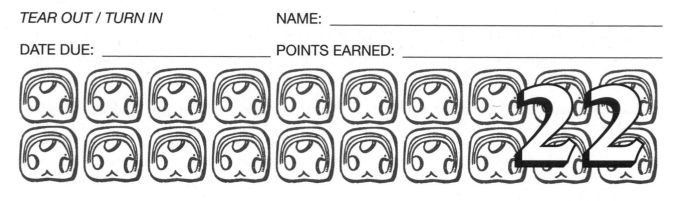

Nonverbal Communication: Space and Touch

The preferred distance between communicators and the types and modes of touch are variables in nonverbal communication. The first exercise presents critical incidents involving proximity of communicators, and the second relates to touch.

Objectives

- To understand how the preferred distance between people communicates nonverbally
- To demonstrate how touch communicates nonverbally

I. Space

Reference

Chapter 10 of text

Instructions

Read each of the three incidents that follow, and for each, choose the alternative you think is the best answer.

1. An American professor of communication is invited to Tokyo to lecture at Aoyama University. Following the lecture, a question-and-answer period is held in a room adjacent to the lecture hall. Refreshments are served. To create an informal atmosphere in the room, the American smiles, pats several students and professors on the back, and says, "Let's be informal. Just call me Don." What will the Japanese do?

    —————— Accept his suggestion and loosen up.

    —————— Become more formal.

    —————— The professors relax; the students remain reticent and deferential.

2. For a class assignment, Debra is invited to work with a foreign student from Saudi Arabia. The girl seems extremely intelligent, and she is one of the few women who have been permitted to study abroad. Their first meeting is in Debra's dorm room, and Debra invites the girl to sit on the only chair while Debra sits on the bed. Instead the girl sits on the bed with Debra, so close that their bodies touch. When she talks, she looks Debra in the eye and touches her frequently. Debra is at a loss, trying to understand the girl's behavior. When they finish, Debra asks the girl to join her for a coke at the campus center. Walking along the campus, the girl holds Debra's hand and later, as they part company the girl embraces Debra and kisses her. Uncomfortable with the relationship, Debra asks the instructor to give her a different partner. What caused the familiarity?

    —————— The girl's nonverbal behavior was sexually oriented.

—————— The girl was behaving in a normal fashion for Arabs.

—————— The girl was overwhelmed with the task they had been assigned and constantly sought comfort from Debra.

3. Mao, a student from the People's Republic of China, meets Walt, an American student, for lunch. As they walk toward the cafeteria, Walt's girlfriend, Barbara, joins them on the way to her next class. Walt and Barbara carry on a lively conversation as they walk arm-in-arm, and they kiss when Barbara leaves them to go to her class. As the two embrace, Mao walks away. When Walt catches up to him, Mao seems cool and distant and goes off to eat by himself. What caused Mao to act in this fashion?

—————— Mao thought it proper to give Walt and Barbara privacy, so he walked away.

—————— Mao was shocked by the outward display of physical affection in public.

—————— Mao was offended by the way Walt and Barbara excluded him from their conversation.

II: Touch

Instructions

Indicate your feelings on the blank by a "C" if you would feel comfortable with this nonverbal expression, "U" if uncomfortable, and "N" if neutral or undecided.

———————   1. Giving/receiving a hug from a same-sex friend.

———————   2. Touching opposite-sex friends.

———————   3. Putting your arm around a same-sex friend.

———————   4. Seeing same-sex persons hugging.

———————   5. Liking opposite-sex persons to touch you.

———————   6. Embracing your date.

———————   7. Getting a back rub from a person of the same sex.

———————   8. Kissing someone of the same sex.

———————   9. Being upset when touched by the opposite sex.

———————   10. Kissing your date.

———————   11. Kissing/embracing relatives of the same sex.

———————   12. Touching opposite-sex individuals intimately.

———————   13. Kissing/embracing relatives of the opposite sex.

———————   14. Showing emotions by touching.

———————   15. Giving a back rub to a person of the same sex.

What Does It Mean?

This exercise is based on Part Three in the text. The answers are on page 85.

I. Match each term with its proper meaning.

_____ 1. Endomorph

_____ 2. Charisma

_____ 3. Phonemes

_____ 4. Bureaucracy

_____ 5. Proxemics

_____ 6. Self-disclosure

_____ 7. Communication apprehension

_____ 8. Conversation

_____ 9. Morpheme

_____ 10. Bernstein

_____ 11. Jiving

_____ 12. Profanity

_____ 13. Immediacy

_____ 14. Kinesics

_____ 15. Adaptors

a. Body movements

b. Unintentional body movements

c. The informal exchange of meanings, feelings, ideas

d. Smallest unit of meaning

e. Revealing intimate information about oneself

f. A level of anxiety associated with talk

g. A hierarchy between the average citizen and the government

h. Referent power

i. Functionally equivalent sounds

j. Restricted and elaborated codes

k. Joking, use of slang, teaching

l. Expletives

m. Closeness

n. Space

o. Oval-shaped

II. Agree ("A") or disagree ("D") with the following statements based on Part Three of the text.

A D   1. A smile does not always indicate pleasure.

A D   2. Clothes are an indicator of the wearer's personality.

A D   3. Looking around while someone is talking probably suggests disinterest.

A D   4. Your facial expression can alter the meaning of what you say.

A D   5. You can imply interest by nodding your head up and down.

A D   6. People often communicate without realizing they are doing so.

A D   7. A person's handshake is a reflection of the person's personality.

A D   8. Slight gestures can carry as much meaning as words.

A D   9. Dissimilar people communicate similar feelings in different ways.

A D   10. The objects on a person's desk can tell much about the person.

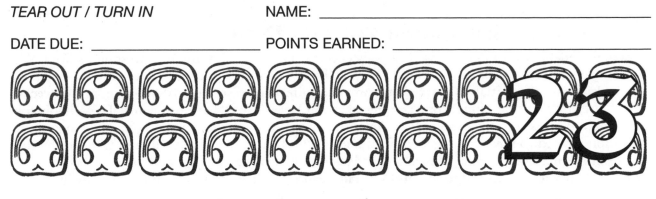

Culture Shock and Acculturation

Case studies are analogies of actual situations, written to reflect the actuality as closely as possible. This exercise consists of three case studies related to culture shock and acculturation. The cases are based on real circumstances.

Objective

• To bring what you have learned in the text into the realm of real life and potential situations

Reference

Chapter 11 of text

Instructions

Read the case studies and be prepared to discuss them in class.

Case One: Teaching in a Foreign Culture

Shortly after her arrival as a teacher of English at Fudan University in Shanghai, Nell Sivad met Joan Mahrog. Joan also taught at Fudan and seemed to enjoy her teaching experience very much, even after several years there. About a month after her arrival, Nell acknowledged problems in her own teaching. She was not succeeding as she had expected. She complained to Joan: "The students don't work very hard, don't do their homework, don't ask questions, and don't do well on exams. I have high standards, and I just don't like teaching here. How can you continue, after all these years, to accept your paycheck with a clear conscience?"

   • What do you think caused Nell's outburst?

   • Was Nell justified in criticizing Joan?

   • Why was Joan succeeding and not Nell?

Case Two: Foreign Student Visits the Doctor

A foreign student from Hong Kong, Hsi, was enrolled in graduate study at a prestigious West Virginia university. From a wealthy family, he had been a brilliant undergraduate student in Hong Kong. Hsi made the initial adjustment to American life with ease and did well for a few weeks, looked after by the local Hong Kong contingent. Soon Hsi began to have problems. The schoolwork was not up to Hsi's standards, and life in America was not all that pleasant for him. The Hong Kong delegation seemed to have gone its own way, and Hsi was left alone. Hsi felt ill and went to the student health center complaining of nausea, headaches, muscle aches, and general listlessness. The doctor prescribed pills, which Hsi took faithfully. His health problems, however, did not go away.

- What was Hsi's problem? Was it his wealthy background — being looked after by servants?
- Was it the lack of support from the Hong Kong group?
- What probably caused his illness?

Case Three: Caucasian in Samoa

Zachary Retlaw went to Samoa to help foster economic development for the people who lived there. Living on the small Pacific island was not easy after life in the big city, and he was the only Caucasian on the island except when the tourists arrived for a day or two. As a consequence, the locals showered him with attention. They catered to his every need — for about three or four months. Then a change took place. No longer did they look after him. In fact, the local people seemed indifferent to him. He grew moody and thought of giving up the development project and returning home.

- What do you think caused the change in people's attitude toward Retlaw?
- Was he just getting tired of the place and ready to go home?
- What could Retlaw do to overcome the people's apparent loss of interest in him?

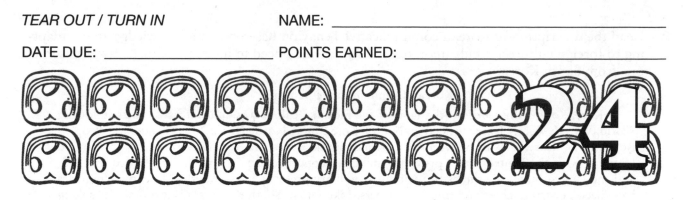

Developing Intercultural Communication Skills

Objective
● To learn how to become a better intercultural communicator

Reference
Chapters 11 and 12 of text

Instructions
1. Think about each of the recommendations in the list below and be prepared to discuss any one or all of them using the text and other literature as a basis.

    1. Respect the right of others to live as they see fit.
    2. Listen to people; empathize with them.
    3. Become adaptable; develop ways of handling uncertainty.
    4. Develop initiative and be willing to take social risks.
    5. Avoid discussing money matters.
    6. Realize that privacy may be lacking in certain cultures.
    7. Recognize the differing roles of women across cultures.
    8. Respect traditions.
    9. Expect and accept long waiting lines.
    10. Avoid discussing politics or imposing your political values on people from other cultures.
    11. Be wary of stereotyping.
    12. Learn the rules of the culture or subculture with which you are interacting.
    13. Develop self-awareness; know your self-image; know what to self-disclose.
    14. Learn the language; observe body language.
    15. When abroad, set aside time for personal rest and relaxation.
    16. Understand your own culture.
    17. Be wary of ridiculing religions; respect the other culture's religion.
    18. Do not look down on another person because of color, creed, or manner of speech.
    19. Respect the attire of people in other cultures.
    20. Make honest attempts to learn and respect the customs of other cultures.

2. Read the description of Korean communicative behavior. Based on your knowledge about adapting to foreign cultures, decide upon the skills you would need to interact competently with someone from South Korea.

Korean Communicative Behavior

Korea, originally *Choson* (the land of the morning calm), was split into two parts following World War II: South Korea (the Republic of Korea) and North Korea (the Democratic People's Republic of Korea). War between North and South Korea led to intervention by the United Nations, with the United States providing military support to the South. The war ended in 1953, and the United States continues to maintain a military presence in the South. These two countries have become strong allies and trading partners. Like Japan, South Korea plays a prominent role in the commercial world of the Pacific Rim, contributing to the vitality of the region. With the birth of the Pacific Century, South Korea is expected to be a major player in world economics.

South Korea's close relationship with the United States has led to intense interest by American educators in its communicative practices. Considerable research clarifies what constitutes a typical Korean communicator.

As a collectivistic society, South Korea stresses harmony, which extends to speaking. Korean harmony is slightly less collectivistic than Japan's. Centuries of subjugation by foreign powers — namely Mongolia, China, and Japan — caused Koreans to attend more closely to individual needs. Attempts were made to support the person as a separate entity in interpersonal relationships, acknowledging his or her personal achievements. Supporting individuals in this manner enhances the group itself and furthers the harmony among group members. Thus, harmony is upheld and collectivism is sustained.

Typical Koreans perceive themselves to be orally active and confident. They portray an attentive, relaxed, and friendly image. Wanting to be in control of communicative situations, they tend to dominate conversations. Nevertheless, they are not open with strangers and do not confide in extended family members. The immediate family hears their innermost concerns.

Typical Koreans are moderately effective in adapting to the needs of those with whom they communicate. Apparently they lack the means or will to adjust their own speaking behavior so it is appropriate in all speaking situations. Even though they are viewed as argumentative, they are not enthusiastic about taking stands on vital issues. Rather, when attacked verbally, they counter with verbal aggressiveness. Although they do not lack assertiveness, they are members of a non-contact society; they do not touch when talking to others. Men, especially, refrain from touching other men. Women avoid public touching of men, although they touch other women in a nonthreatening manner and without sexual overtones.

Interacting with people from other cultures, Koreans should hold their own — provided that they know the language spoken. In a heated exchange with Americans, they will not win friends and, if aggressive Koreans confront argumentative Americans, enmity surely will develop.

To interact competently with a typical Korean, I would adjust my speech behavior by doing this:

_____

_____

_____

I would use these skills: _____

_____

_____

_____

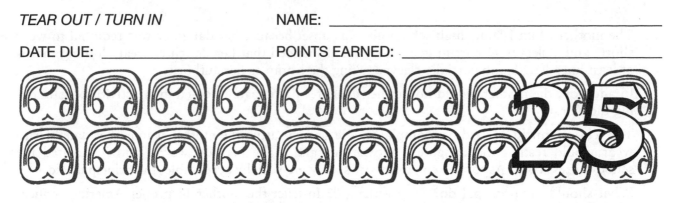

Becoming Culturally Aware in the Classroom

The classroom of today is multicultural, and the varied cultural backgrounds of the students present the teachers with a multitude of challenges, as the following cases illustrate.

Objective

● To use what you have learned in this course to become more culturally aware

Reference

Text

Instructions

Answer the questions and offer solutions, taking into consideration cultural differences, yet being fair to all students.

1. Professor Richman's communication class has 250 students — including 10 from Japan, 25 from Mexico, and 12 from other countries. Her examinations generally take an entire class period — if the students write fast.

   None of the Japanese finished the first exam, and half of the Mexicans and those from other countries did. All of the Americans finished on time. The Japanese answers were correct. Of course, they didn't finish, so they flunked, as did the Mexicans and those from the other cultures. All believed that, given enough time, they would have passed.

   Richman's response was that all students were treated equally; all had the same amount of time to complete the exam. It would not be fair to the Americans, she argued, if the foreign students were given more time, even though their English comprehension was weak, requiring them to look up words in their pocket dictionaries.

   The administration took a hands-off attitude because the issue involved the professor's academic freedom. What are your reactions to the professor's response? To the administration's? Were they insensitive to the foreign students' plight? Should foreign students be given the same treatment as the Americans? If so, why? If not, why not? How would you handle the situation? Is fairness an issue in these circumstances?

2. The mother of an Islamic high-school girl was upset because her daughter was required to wear shorts and a sleeveless shirt in gym class. She demanded that her daughter wear clothing that is at least knee-length and partially sleeved, citing the Koran as her authority.

In addition, the mother would not let her daughter participate in co-ed gym activities, again citing the Koran.

The school principal heard her complaints. He said the attire the mother wanted her daughter to wear would restrict the daughter's movements and make her too warm, and it violated the school's dress code. As for the co-ed activities, they are socially acceptable, the principal said.

What should the principal do? Excuse the girl? Instruct the mother in proper American educational practices? Provide private instruction for the girl? Let the girl wear what the Koran allows?

How would you solve this problem?

3. Upon graduation with her bachelor's degree in education, Julie began teaching in the local secondary school. Her subject area was home economics. An important part of the home economics curriculum was to teach the students how to prepare meals, including meat dishes. Julie bought cheap cuts of beef and pork for the students in her cooking lab.

After receiving the instructions on how to prepare the meat, one student told her that eating meat is sinful. Beef and pork come from animals, and killing cows and pigs or anything else is sinful. Meat eaters are as bad as people who kill other people. Another student said that eating pork was against her religion. Still another said the same thing about beef.

How can Julie deal with these cultural issues? Should she continue the instruction? Eliminate the meat dishes? How can she handle the cultural problems regarding food without discontinuing the class entirely?

How should she solve the problem?

? What Does It Mean?

These phrases are used in Part Four in the text. The answers are on page 85.

Match the phrase with the appropriate meaning.

_____ 1. The honeymoon is over.

_____ 2. People supposedly think and act as we do.

_____ 3. Indiscrimination.

_____ 4. Everyone blends into one.

_____ 5. The culture one joins.

_____ 6. Learning and adjusting to new behaviors in a new culture.

_____ 7. Seeing the world as the speaker sees it.

_____ 8. Generalized trauma affecting people in a new and different culture.

_____ 9. Ability to maintain a positive state of mind.

_____ 10. Maintenance of separate and distinct cultural entities.

a. Participant stage

b. Projective cognitive similarity

c. Stereotyping

d. Melting pot

e. Host

f. Acculturation

g. Empathy

h. Culture shock

i. Emotional resilience

j. Cultural pluralism

Answers to "What Does It Mean?"

Part III of Exercise 3: All the statements are false; the answers all disagree.

Following Exercise 5

1. h
2. b
3. e
4. j
5. f
6. g
7. d
8. c
9. i
10. a

Following Exercise 12

Statements 2, 8, and 9 are false in the first section. The remaining answers are true. The answers to the second part are:

1. h
2. e
3. d
4. i
5. f
6. a
7. b
8. c
9. j
10. g

Following Exercise 16

I. Items 4, 5, and 10 are true. The others are false.

II:
1. e
2. c
3. d
4. j
5. f
6. h
7. i
8. b
9. g
10. a

III.
1. h
2. c
3. b
4. i
5. g
6. j
7. f
8. d
9. e
10. a

Following Exercise 22

I.
1. o
2. h
3. i
4. g
5. n
6. e
7. f
8. c
9. d
10. j
11. k
12. l
13. m
14. a
15. b

II. All agree.

Following Exercise 25

1. a
2. b
3. c
4. d
5. e
6. f
7. g
8. h
9. i
10. j

EXAM NUMBER: _____   NAME: _____

POINTS EARNED: _____

ANSWER SHEET

[Use for short answer and essay type exams. Write legibly.]

EXAM NUMBER: _____   NAME: _____

POINTS EARNED: _____

ANSWER SHEET

[Use for short answer and essay type exams. Write legibly.]

EXAM NUMBER: _____ NAME: _____

POINTS EARNED: _____

ANSWER SHEET

[Use for short answer and essay type exams. Write legibly.]

EXAM NUMBER: _____   NAME: _____

POINTS EARNED: _____

ANSWER SHEET

[Use for short answer and essay type exams. Write legibly.]

EXAM NUMBER: _____   NAME: _____

POINTS EARNED: _____

ANSWER SHEET

[Use for short answer and essay type exams. Write legibly.]

EXAM NUMBER: _____ NAME: _____

POINTS EARNED: _____

ANSWER SHEET

	T 1	F 2	3	4	5		1	2	3	4	5		T 1	F 2	3	4	5		T 1	F 2	3	4	5		T 1	F 2	3	4	5
1						24						47						70						93					
2						25						48						71						94					
3						26						49						72						95					
4						27						50						73						96					
5						28						51						74						97					
6						29						52						75						98					
7						30						53						76						99					
8						31						54						77						100					
9						32						55						78											
10						33						56						79											
11						34						57						80											
12						35						58						81											
13						36						59						82											
14						37						60						83											
15						38						61						84											
16						39						62						85											
17						40						63						86											
18						41						64						87											
19						42						65						88											
20						43						66						89											
21						44						67						90											
22						45						68						91											
23						46						69						92											

EXAM NUMBER: _____   NAME: _____

POINTS EARNED: _____

ANSWER SHEET

	T 1	F 2	3	4	5
1					
2					
3					
4					
5					
6					
7					
8					
9					
10					
11					
12					
13					
14					
15					
16					
17					
18					
19					
20					
21					
22					
23					

	T 1	F 2	3	4	5
24					
25					
26					
27					
28					
29					
30					
31					
32					
33					
34					
35					
36					
37					
38					
39					
40					
41					
42					
43					
44					
45					
46					

	T 1	F 2	3	4	5
47					
48					
49					
50					
51					
52					
53					
54					
55					
56					
57					
58					
59					
60					
61					
62					
63					
64					
65					
66					
67					
68					
69					

	T 1	F 2	3	4	5
70					
71					
72					
73					
74					
75					
76					
77					
78					
79					
80					
81					
82					
83					
84					
85					
86					
87					
88					
89					
90					
91					
92					

	T 1	F 2	3	4	5
93					
94					
95					
96					
97					
98					
99					
100					

EXAM NUMBER: _____ NAME: _____

POINTS EARNED: _____

ANSWER SHEET

	T 1	F 2	3	4	5			T 1	F 2	3	4	5			T 1	F 2	3	4	5			T 1	F 2	3	4	5			T 1	F 2	3	4	5
1							24							47							70							93					
2							25							48							71							94					
3							26							49							72							95					
4							27							50							73							96					
5							28							51							74							97					
6							29							52							75							98					
7							30							53							76							99					
8							31							54							77							100					
9							32							55							78												
10							33							56							79												
11							34							57							80												
12							35							58							81												
13							36							59							82												
14							37							60							83												
15							38							61							84												
16							39							62							85												
17							40							63							86												
18							41							64							87												
19							42							65							88												
20							43							66							89												
21							44							67							90												
22							45							68							91												
23							46							69							92												

EXAM NUMBER: _____   NAME: _____

POINTS EARNED: _____

ANSWER SHEET

A bubble answer grid with questions numbered 1–100, each offering columns labeled T (1), F (2), 3, 4, 5.

	T 1	F 2	3	4	5		T 1	F 2	3	4	5		T 1	F 2	3	4	5		T 1	F 2	3	4	5		T 1	F 2	3	4	5
1						24						47						70						93					
2						25						48						71						94					
3						26						49						72						95					
4						27						50						73						96					
5						28						51						74						97					
6						29						52						75						98					
7						30						53						76						99					
8						31						54						77						100					
9						32						55						78											
10						33						56						79											
11						34						57						80											
12						35						58						81											
13						36						59						82											
14						37						60						83											
15						38						61						84											
16						39						62						85											
17						40						63						86											
18						41						64						87											
19						42						65						88											
20						43						66						89											
21						44						67						90											
22						45						68						91											
23						46						69						92											

EXAM NUMBER: _____   NAME: _____

POINTS EARNED: _____

ANSWER SHEET

	T	F						T	F						T	F						T	F						T	F			
	1	2	3	4	5			1	2	3	4	5			1	2	3	4	5			1	2	3	4	5			1	2	3	4	5	
1							24							47							70							93						
2							25							48							71							94						
3							26							49							72							95						
4							27							50							73							96						
5							28							51							74							97						
6							29							52							75							98						
7							30							53							76							99						
8							31							54							77							100						
9							32							55							78													
10							33							56							79													
11							34							57							80													
12							35							58							81													
13							36							59							82													
14							37							60							83													
15							38							61							84													
16							39							62							85													
17							40							63							86													
18							41							64							87													
19							42							65							88													
20							43							66							89													
21							44							67							90													
22							45							68							91													
23							46							69							92													